THE CREATIVE ENCOUNTER

An Interpretation of Religion and the Social Witness

By HOWARD THURMAN

RICHMOND
INDIANA

THE CREATIVE ENCOUNTER

Published by arrangement with the author.
Harper & Row edition published, 1954.
Friends United Press edition published, 1972.
© , 1954, by Harper & Brothers

Printed in the U.S.A. by Prinit Press, Dublin, IN

For further information address Friends United Press, 101 Quaker Hill Drive, Richmond, Indiana 47374.

International Standard Book No. 0-913408-07-7
Library of Congress Catalog Card No. 72-12773

TO COLEMAN JENNINGS

Friend and companion in the Way

AUTHOR'S NOTE

THE substance of these pages, in essentially the present form, was given as the Merrick Lectures at Ohio Wesleyan University in March, 1954. In accordance with the spirit of the establishing of the lectureship, the lectures deal with an aspect of "experimental and practical religion."

It is a privilege to record my appreciation to the administration, faculty and student body of Ohio Wesleyan University for the courtesies which they extended to Mrs. Thurman and me while we were guests on their campus.

A special word of appreciation to Miss Margaret Harding, Secretary of Marsh Chapel, for her efficient handling of many details in the preparation of this volume; to Miss Sydna Altschuler, who typed and retyped the manuscript, and to those several persons with whom the lectures were discussed and who gave many pointed suggestions.

THE PAPERBACK EDITION

This paperback edition of The Creative Encounter *is a response to many requests. At a time when there is mounting interest in the experience of meditation, it is a unique opportunity to call attention to the imperious demand that a rhythmic balance be maintained between the inner and the outer life which make a single pulse beat of the spiritual and ethical demand.*

San Francisco
September, 1972

PREFACE

MODERN American man tends to be ashamed of his feelings. To feel deeply is to seem emotional, sentimental, weak. The rumor abounds that feelings are vapid, vague, escape hatches for the human spirit. There is a widespread insistence upon objectivity in observation, thinking, and living. Hence to feel is to become subjective and therefore to act without the objectivity of responsibility; it is to do violence to rational process. Lewis Mumford has given expression to a phrase descriptive of this modern temper: "There is no alternative between frigidity and panic." How to feel, and at the same time be intellectually self-respecting, makes for real conflict.

It is the purpose of this volume to give an interpretation of the meaning of religious experience as it involves the individual, totally, which means inclusive of feelings and emotions. Further, its purpose is to examine, somewhat, the effect that such experience has upon the complete life of the individual, both as a private person and as a member of society. The first chapter discusses the inwardness of religion or religious experience as an inner process or more accurately as an inner event or series of events. A working definition of the meaning of religious experience is set forth as an encounter between man and God, the two principals involved in the experience itself. There follows an examination of at least two disciplines that are fruitful in preparing the spirit of man for the encounter. The two disciplines outlined are prayer and human suffering.

The second chapter deals with the outwardness of religion or the bearing that the encounter has upon the personal, private context of meaning in which the individual lives and by which his life is defined. Outwardness is first interpreted as the

result in the life of the individual's nervous structure and pattern of behavior derived from the impact of the religious experience. Here we are
involved with the mechanics of the surrender of
the life to God. The difference comes because of a
basic shift in centeredness. It is here that the new
life takes hold and spreads its influence through all
of living. Of such is the root of the new motivation
resulting from the encounter with God in the religious experience.

The third chapter discusses the relationship between the ordinary human need for love from the
beginning of infancy and the grand fulfillment of
the personality in the experience of the love of
God. It is here that the full-orbed vitality of feelings fertilizes the total personality and nourishes
the very roots of being. Genuineness of motive
must be matched with integrity of feelings—all in
the presence of God in the religious experience.

The final chapter deals with the outer necessity
for love in the social relations which are part and
parcel of the individual's experience of community.

There is no attempt to examine the implications in their bearing upon a variety of relations in the social structure. A passing reference is made to the significance of civic responsibility and character growing out of the inner demand for love. The crux of this aspect of the discussion treats of the religious institution as the place in which love in all its meanings would be fostered as a result of the religious experience of which the institution is officially the trustee. It is on this point that the challenge rests.

To sum up, there is no attempt to present a technical interpretation of the meaning, definition, or place of religious experience for the formal scholar of religious phenomena. The literature in this field is definitive, if not altogether adequate.

This volume is the testimony of a personal quest with many indications of seeking and perhaps little evidence of finding. No claim is made other than that of one who, despite fumblings, errors, and grave shortcomings, senses that

. . . to KNOW

Rather consists in opening out a way
  Whence the imprisoned splendour may escape,
  Than in effecting entry for a light
  Supposed to be without.

HOWARD THURMAN

15

THE CREATIVE ENCOUNTER

I   THE INWARDNESS OF RELIGION

AS A person each of us lives a private life; there is
a world within where for us the great issues of our
lives are determined. It is here that at long last the
"yea" and "nay" of our living is defined, declared.
It is private. It is cut off from immediate involvement in what surrounds us. It is my world. This
does not suggest, nor is it meant to suggest, that it
is merely the creation of my own mind, thought,
and imagination. True, I am a child not only of
nature, of parents, but also I am a child of my
nation, which in turn makes me a child of my civilization and the culture whose roots finally mingle
with other cultures and civilizations long since
passed into history. But there remains a private,
personal world which I claim as uniquely my own.

Religious experience is interpreted to mean the conscious and direct exposure of the individual to God. Such an experience seems to the individual to be inclusive of all the meaning of his life—there is nothing that is not involved. There is present here what William James refers to as "acquaintance-knowledge" as contrasted with "knowledge about." It is immediate experience and yet experience that is purely immediate is not quite possible. The individual is never an isolated, independent unit. He brings to his religious experience certain structural and ideological equipment or tools. This equipment is apt to be very determinative in how he interprets the significance not only of his religious experience but also the significance of experience itself.

It is a rather curious paradox, and yet not altogether curious this idea, this fact rather, that the individual is very importantly an experiencer. All of the details of his experience, that is, the raw materials of his experience, are in some very crucial manner worked over by him, assimilated by him, and thus they become parts of what he defines as his own person, his own personality, or his own self. But the individual is never completely one with his experiences. He remains always observer and participant. This is very important to remember. To clarify it at this point is crucial for our discussion.

Several years ago I had the privilege of spending a full day in informal discussion with Kshiti Mohan Sen who, at the time, was the head of the Division of Oriental Studies at Santeneketan, Tagore's university in North India. Doctor Sen was one of the great authorities on medieval mysticism in Hinduism. At the end of our morning's conversation, as I arose to go to keep a luncheon appointment with some students on campus, I found myself smiling inwardly; as I thought. Doctor Sen noted the fact that I was amused, at the very moment that I noticed that he was amused also. "I see you're smiling. I think we're smiling about the same thing," he said. "I think so," was my reply. "Suppose you tell me first," he said. Then I said,

"I was thinking how much time we have wasted sparring for position—you from behind your Hindu breastwork, and I from behind my Christian embankment. Occasionally we peered out at each other to be sure that each was somehow in sight of the other." "Quite right," he said and continuing, "Let's be wiser when we return this afternoon." When our discussion resumed, we were able to communicate with each other in a manner that was for me profound and completely unique. In one sweeping assumption I gathered up in my thinking his *Hindu fact* and for me he did essentially the same with my *Christian fact*. We were thus released to communicate with each other as sharers of what each in his own way had discovered of his experience of God. We were no longer under the necessity to defend anything but were free to be to each other what was most fundamental to each.

In authentic religious experience the individual is himself totally involved. This involvement includes the context of meanings, experiences, and

so may my preaching! theology

values by which the *persona* is defined. He does not come into the experience *de novo,* but rather does the individual come into the Presence of God with the smell of life upon him. As Mr. Valiant-for-Truth in *Pilgrim's Progress* states it as he crosses over the river Jordan:

> My sword I give to him that shall succeed me in my pilgrimage, and my courage and skill to him that can get them. My marks and scars I carry with me to be a witness for me that I have fought his battles who will now be my rewarder.

Nevertheless, there is present in religious experience an original and direct element which seems to be in, and of itself, intrinsic and supremely worthful. By this original and direct element, I do not mean some special religious organ or some unique religious element in the personality. But there is the aspect *extraordinary* in religious experience. But what?

It is in order to seek an answer to this question. The central fact in religious experience is the awareness of meeting God. The descriptive words used are varied: sometimes it is called an encounter; sometimes, a confrontation; and sometimes, a sense of Presence. What is insisted upon, however, without regard to the term used, is that in the experience defined as religious, the individual is seen as being exposed to direct knowledge of ultimate meaning, *ne plus ultra* being, in which all that the individual is, becomes clear as immediate and often distinct revelation. He is face to face with something which is so much more, and so much more inclusive, than all of his awareness of himself that for him, *in the moment,* there are no questions. Without asking, somehow he knows.

The mind apprehends the whole—the experience is beyond or inclusive of the discursive. It is not other than the discursive, but somehow it is inclusive of the discursive. As Bennett puts it, "It is the knowledge of the subject of all predicates." It is precisely because of this synoptic apprehension that the individual in the experience seems to come into possession of what he has known as being true all along. The thing that is new is the *realization.* And this is of profound importance.

Several years ago I spent about ten days with a group of students at Pawling, New York. One afternoon I stretched out on the grass to read a book. It was a beautiful day with light blue clouds floating aimlessly against the background of sky that was of much deeper blue. Presently a friend came by. He chatted for a few minutes and then as he was leaving he looked up in the sky and said, "Look, look at the cloud formation, Howard, what does it look like to you?" I gazed thoughtfully and then I said, "I don't know. I've been looking at it intermittently for the past thirty minutes, but it does not remind me of anything in particular—I don't think." "Shame on you," he said. "It looks just like the bust of George Washington." And surely enough it did. Nothing had changed except that now there was added a new dimension of awareness of what I had been looking at for some time but had not seen. Realization was added and that made the difference.

In religious experience the *realization* makes the difference. What is the nature of such realization and/or of what is it a realization? For the

Christian there are two principals in, or parties to,
the religious experience. One is the individual
himself, and the other is God, or for many
Christians the term Christ would be used. There
are then two principals, parties, or persons central
in or to the drama of religious experience. As has
been pointed out, the individual is inclusive of his
totality, which must of necessity carry with it the
pattern and contents of his belief, his value judgments, his strengths, and his weaknesses; in fine,
the total person as defined to himself by himself.

Included in this totality is what the individual
means by the term God. This preliminary residue
of God-meaning, however it may be defined, is
the starting point of communication between the
two principals in the religious experience. It is at
this point that the meaning of the experience takes
hold. Initially, it cannot be more than this or it
would be meaningless; it cannot be less than this or
it would be utterly unworthy.

In many ways Jesus illustrated this basic insight
concerning how God relates to man. The parable

of the man who hired the workers at different times during the day and paid them all the same wages is but to mention only one instance. There must be a conscious "toe hold" for God in religious experience. A friend of mine was having great difficulty because he could not establish any authentic basis of communication with his landlady. He observed one day that her idea of a gentleman was one who kept the ash trays empty of cigarettes and dead matches. He resolved to keep his ash trays empty not only in his own room, but also to make a habit of emptying ash trays wherever he saw that they needed emptying, whenever he came through the living room. It worked like magic—a basis of communication was established now which eventually led to understanding at many levels of appreciation. *He met her at the level of the ash trays.* In religious experience God meets the individual at the level not only of the individual's needs, but also, in my judgment more incisively, at the level of his residue of God-meaning and goes forward from there.

It is in order to examine the residue of God-meaning. There seems always to be a two-dimensional demand that is inherent in this residue of God-meaning. The first dimension is that God must be all-inclusive, all-comprehending, and in a profound sense universal. This means that God is not merely the Creator of creatures, of all objects animate and inanimate; but also, and more importantly, that God is the Creator of life itself. Existence is the creation of God; life is the creation of God. This is of more than passing significance. The effort is to provide some kind of crucial rationale for the aliveness of life. We are, all of us, impressed with the fact that there is what is defined as a living quality present in all living things. For instance, when we say that a thing or a person or an animal is alive, we mean something in particular. It is characterized by a definite kind of recognized behavior which in our thought distinguishes a dead thing from a living thing. This is one of the most impressive facts about living objects. We are so overwhelmed by the personal but vast impact of the particularity of living objects that we are scarcely aware of a much more profound fact in our midst and that is that life itself is alive. It is the quality of aliveness that bottoms and sustains all of the welter and variety of particular manifestations. Hence my dog, Kropotkin, will die. My friend's dog, Dukie, will die; but dogs will not die. Dogs keep coming on. There is a quality of livingness that would indicate that life itself is eternal in this sense. (Perhaps this is a partial explanation of the fact that living things are sustained by consuming living things.) Here we are dealing with a subject of which all living things themselves are predicate. This subject quality of life seems always to be previous in time to all particular living things or all particular manifestations. Hence in Israel, God is not only Creator but in the prayers of Judaism is often referred to as the King of the universe.

In sum, the encounter with God, if it is to be satisfying, must be with One who is seen as holding within His context all that there is, including existence itself. This provides an ultimate point of reference for the final fact of experience of whatever character altogether. The significance of the assurance cannot possibly be overestimated. It suggests that here the human spirit is exposed to the kind of experience that is capable of providing an ultimate clue to all levels of reality, to all the dimensions of time, and to all aspects of faith and the manifestations therein. If there is to be found anywhere an ultimate dependence on the fact of integrity, this is it. The individual, if he is assured in such an encounter, has the confidence of ultimate security. Such is the first demand that is made upon religious experience as defined.

But all of this involves the individual only as a living object in the world of living objects. Such assurance as we described is at long last impersonal. There is no quality that is personal in terms of unique value. The integrity is in the divine object. The advertising slogan of a famous pharmaceutical house is this, "The integrity of the maker is the priceless ingredient." Such assurance

however is metaphysical in character and belongs
in the category of impersonal assurance. But in the
religious experience there must be something
more.

The second demand is that the encounter be
with Someone who is capable of dealing personally and privately with the individual. The
human spirit seems inherently allergic to isolation.
It cannot abide a sense of being permanently alone
or stranded in all the vastness of the universe or
lost in the midst of the complexities of personal
experiences. We cannot finally abide being
ignored. When our older daughter was about two
years old, she was spending a few days with my
sister. One day, without any apparent reason or
provocation, she decided to fight my sister. Steadily
and determinedly she was ignored. Finally she
burst out in tears, saying to my sister, "Why don't
you fight me back?" In other words—"Crush me,
overpower me, but do not ignore me." Strangely
enough and parenthetically, very often the measure
which we place upon our own significance is the

amount of power that must be used in order to overcome us. Deep within there is the need for recognition, for being personally regarded that persists and permits of no substitute. We shall return to this basic concept later in our discussion. Suffice it to say here that one demand that is made upon religious experience is that it be private, personal, individual, and therefore unique. It is never sufficient for the individual to have a clue merely to ultimate significance in general, but there must be provided in the religious experience a sense of the ultimate worth of the individual himself as a private person.

In the light of the above considerations, religious experience provides a meeting point between the two principals—God and man. This is the only basis upon which an effective communication between the principals can be established.

We now turn to an examination of the nature of the experience and what may be learned from it. The first observation is that such an experience is not casual. It may arise in a context that is not

directive, a context that may have all the characteristics of the permissive. A man may be faced with
this in the sudden turning of the road. The
incidents of his life may, without a moment's
notice, catapult him into the midst of the experience which is completely irradiated with the presence of God. In any wilderness the unsuspecting
traveler may come upon the burning bush, and
discover that the ground upon which he stands is
holy ground. Wherever such occurs, we may be
sure that even though the context itself may be
casual or even random, the experience itself is not.

Again it is to be observed that the experience
always has in it a volitional element. The self is
active in it. Even when a man is in deep conflict
which results in his fleeing from what is a great
urgency within him, he is always involved and
the moral quality of will is present. All of this
means that there must be a very special kind of
preparation. The preparation involves much of
what is meant by spiritual discipline.

The central discipline for our purposes is prayer.

It is apart from my intention to discuss the efficacy of prayer, the different kinds of prayer, and the fearful complexities of intercessory prayer. It is relevant to my purpose to discuss the aspect of prayer that throws light on the meaning of primary religious experience.

In the first place prayer, in the sense in which I am using it, means the *method* by which the individual makes his way to the temple of quiet within his own spirit and the *activity* of his spirit within its walls. Prayer is not only the participation in communication with God in the encounter of religious experience, but it is also the "readying" of the spirit for such communication. It is the total process of quieting down and to that extent must not be separated from meditation. Perhaps, as important as prayer itself, is the "readying" of the spirit for the experience.

In such "readying" a quiet place is very important if not altogether mandatory. In the noise of our times such a place may be impossible to find. One of the great services that the Christian church can render to the community is to provide spells and spaces of quiet for the world-weary men and women whose needs are so desperate. When I was a minister at Oberlin many years ago, I noted that one of my most active parishioners in the life of the church always went to sleep a few minutes after the sermon began. Her embarrassment was evident. One day when I went by to see her husband who was ill, she took me aside to apologize for sleeping during the sermon. I took in the total situation in which she lived—it was the noisiest household I think I have ever seen. I said to her that the church rendered her a distinct service if it provided her with a quiet place, in inspiring surroundings, at eleven o'clock in the morning, in which she could have a few moments of deep relaxing sleep. In much more important ways the church can contribute to the quiet place for the "readying" process.

In addition to the quiet place, one must turn inward away from the things in the mind that divide and scatter one's thoughts and indeed one's spirit. There are many helpful suggestions along this line. Of course, there must be the felt need for withdrawal, for turning aside; such a need is commonplace, even though it may not be associated always with any kind of religious experience. There is no greater preparation in the "readying" process than the quiet reading from the Bible, particularly the devotional Psalms or the Gospels wherein Jesus is expressing his love for someone. There are many other inspiring records left by men who were able to put into timeless prose or inspired verse the things they heard as they listened in the Way. It is as important, if not more so, to quiet the inner noises than to isolate oneself from the outer noises.

Again one may find it extremely helpful to discover a "clothesline" on which all of one's feelings and thoughts and desires may be placed. It may be a simple sentence like the great organ note with which the 139th Psalm opens, "O Lord, thou hast searched me, and known me. Thou knowest my downsitting and mine uprising, thou understandest my thought afar off." Or it may be some long forgotten but now subtly recalled line from a hymn or a phrase from a prayer heard at another period. It may be some incident which disclosed a wink of reality that will set the stage. Sometimes focusing is impossible because of some carking anxiety or deep hurt or unrelieved guilt or shame that will not let one go. If such be the case, then, use the snare as the "readying" point. This is the meaning of the line from the hymn, "And sanctify to Thee thy deepest distress." Often the focusing of the mind upon some phase of the life of the Master will fill the whole being with irradiation, and one finds one's way to the very presence of God.

When one has been thus prepared, a strange thing happens. It is very difficult to put into words. The initiative slips out of one's hands and into the hands of God, the other Principal in the religious experience. The self moves toward God. Such movement seems to have the quality of innate and fundamental stirring. The self does not see itself as being violated, though it may be challenged, stimulated, inspired, conditioned, but all of this takes place in a frame of reference that is completely permissive. There is another movement which is at once merged with the movement of the self. God touches the spirit and the will and a wholly new character in terms of dimension enters the experience. In this sense prayer may be regarded as an open-end experience.

Fundamental to the total fact of prayer in the Christian religion is the persuasive affirmation that the God of religious experience is a seeking and a beseeching God. "O Jerusalem, Jerusalem, . . . how often would I have gathered thy children together, even as a hen gathereth her chickens under her wings, and ye would not." The great parables of "The Lost Sheep," "The Lost Coin," and "The Prodigal Son" carry the same idea. The discovery of such a fact in one's experience in life is first met in the religious experience itself.

A friend of mine sent me a quotation from her professor who gave to her class a talk on faith and prayer. The quotation is as follows:

The Secret Temple is the place of meditation. There is need for such a temple in every man's soul and need for the setting apart of some portion of each day that we may enter the sacred edifice and, in that holy place, undefiled by the intrusion of the world, may renew our ideals, make clear our purposes and enlighten our wills by the religious vision. Even though the form of our prayer be petition, at least one of its functions is the defining of our ideals in the light of the widest perspectives available to us, and our voluntary alliance with purposes of the highest worth. It is only in the Secret Temple or in the presence of our God that we discover and strengthen our truest selves.

Religious experience in its profoundest dimension is the finding of man by God and the finding of God by man. This is the inner witness. The moral quality is mandatory because the individual must be genuine in his preparation and in his motivation and in his response. His faith must be active and dynamic. It was pointed out earlier that the individual enters the experience and/or the preparation for it with the smell of life heavy upon him. He has in him all his errors and blindness, his raw conscience and his scar tissues, all his loves and hates. In fact, all that he is as he lives life is with him in this experience. It is in his religious experience that he sees himself from another point of view. In a very real sense he is stripped of everything and he stands with no possible protection from the countenance of the Other. The things of which he is stripped are not thrown away. They are merely laid aside and with infinite patience they are seen for what they are. It is here that the great decision is made as to what will be kept and what will be discarded. A man may take a whole lifetime to put away a particular garment forever. The new center is found, and it is often like giving birth to a new self. It is small wonder that so much is made in the Christian religion of the necessity of rebirths. There need not be only one single rebirth, but again and again a man may be reborn until at last there is nothing that remains between him and God.

We have postponed as long as possible the crucial question which religious experience must undertake to answer. Does such an experience yield knowledge about the two principals in the experience? The point does not have to be labored that for the individual much is revealed about himself, his aims, his purposes, his desires. Here in the religious experience itself a man begins to understand what manner of man he truly is and what it is that he undertakes to define with his life as the meaning of his enterprise. Changes in him do take place and these changes can be duly noted by a series of observable data which are a part of his subsequent living. He can observe gradual or sometimes apparent shifts in his total pattern. This is particularly true in the traditional conversion experience in evangelical Christianity, but such experiences are a dramatic manifestation of what I am regarding as the characteristic of regular religious experience, the normal living pattern of the religious man. It is true that a man may look back over his life to discover that his life has been

molded and reshaped by the effects deep within
him of the constant exposure of his life to God
in his religious experience. Through the years he
has brought to his experience the burdens of his
life; he has shared with it his deepest joys and
profoundest concerns, and all of this for him has
made a difference.

But what about knowledge of the other Principal, God? Does the religious experience yield any
knowledge of God or is that which is experienced
here the data of knowledge? If central to the
religious experience is the recognition of God as
being the Creator of life and existence, then He
must, in a very definite manner, stand over against
creation. He is the subject and all existences are
predicates. What is the relation between God and
His creatures? Is He wholly transcendent? Such
would satisfy the demands of creation, but would
it satisfy the demands of religious experience? No.
The crucial element in religious experience, as one
thinks of it, is some form of personal communion
between the two principals, man and God. This

means that either the soul of man must be regarded as a very part of God or else some other means must be devised or projected so as to make authentic communication between man and God possible. It is the claim of religious experience, as defined, that such connection does take place. Man and God do communicate. It is not necessary to take the position of the most radical mystic in order to satisfy the demands of the religious experience at this point. Eckhart insists that there is in the soul of man an apex, a spark which is God, the Godhead. This is the very ground of the soul. It is in and of itself the Godhead. It follows quite logically then that the only thing that keeps God from filling the soul completely is what Eckhart refers to as creatureliness. For it is his insistence that if man is emptied of creatureliness, then God has no alternative but to fill him up—if He does that, there is no difference then between God and man except in the rather tenuous boundaries of the self. It is possible, however, that there may be an identity of purposes both discernible and discoverable which would be the meeting point for communication. This is a part of the meaning of the large place that the will of God has in the warp and woof of Christian thought. In the experience of religion I may learn somewhat of the will of God and yield my own private, personal will to His will and thereby gain insight into purposes that transcend my little purposes and meanings that transcend or extend far beyond the reach of my own little meanings.

Of course, there can be no communication unless there is some common ground or some common meeting point. Such a meeting point may be in essence or in structure or in experience. Fundamental to our thinking is the concept that God is the Creator of life and the Creator of man, and this in itself would tend to indicate that, therefore, God and man initially have that in common which the creature would have in common with the Creator. The place at which this contention seems to be relevant is at the point of the concern and the interest which the individual has for sharing in and creating values. It is quite conceivable that if there are purposes in the mind of the Creator and if I may enter into fellowship and communication with the Creator, then I would as a result of that fellowship and communication be exposed to the vision of His purposes. The degree to which I respond to that vision do I participate formally and consciously in those purposes. Thus my commitment becomes one in which I put at the disposal of the larger and more creative purposes of the Creator my little life, my little thoughts, my little activities, my little devotions. In the living of my life I establish more and more levels of understanding of the Creator as I achieve in fact what I see in vision.

What then does religious experience teach us about God? The most important thing that it teaches us is that God is. This is not an inference, but it is a disclosure. Perhaps I should say this is not merely an inference, but it is also a disclosure. He who comes to God must believe that He is—thus the Evangel puts it. The knowledge is immediate, direct, and is not an inference from logic and the "therefore" of a syllogism. The firsthand knowledge of God is always in the nature of revelation. It is an awareness of literal truth directly perceived. Such is the testimony of religious experience. We may disagree with it or even sit in judgment upon it, but it cannot be disputed unless one stands within the framework of the experience itself, and to do that is to share the witness.

There is something about the soul of man that includes in its very structure this intuitive knowledge. Intuition is not spontaneous, despite the fact that it seems to be so. There is a moment in all intuition which is deeply rooted in the data with reference to which the intuition is relevant. Intuition is like a running broad jump. The runner dashes a certain number of feet down the cinder path until he comes to the threshold of the sand pit—at this point he leaps into the air and is carried forward by the momentum created by the speed and drive which are his in the cinder path.

There is a "leaping quality" which simply utilizes to the full the momentum that is in direct line with it. There is in all intuition the element of revelation which may be characterized as the leaping element. This aspect of intuition makes it throw light on known materials; and the thing that makes it an intuition is the fact that it establishes clearly and definitely what was known peripherally, vaguely, or merely dimly sensed. The intuition says that I bring you knowledge which has been there and in you all along. Such intuition serves a very important purpose in religious experience for it is the intuition that finally takes on a molding and tutoring character which gives content, in terms of concept, to the body of belief which becomes the individual's religious equipment. It must be kept in mind that, how the person relates the intuition to the context of his life so that it becomes a handle by which he is able to connect himself with the living world of living events, is determined by the equipment which he brings to the experience.

There is at least one other discipline aside from prayer that may contribute significantly to the meaning not only of religious experience but may throw light upon both principals in the religious experience. I refer to human suffering. Suffering *may* prepare the spirit in the same manner that characterizes meditation as a preparation for the religious experience. It is true that suffering sets up one of the roadblocks to religious experience. There are two spiritual problems created by suffering—one is the actual pain, discomfort and frustration itself. The normal process of life has been interrupted, and the sufferer is faced with what seems a great irrationality. The pain brings one face to face with the point at which evil touches him in particular. At such a time the problem of evil is robbed of its speculative detachment and becomes personal indeed. The problem of evil becomes a bed-ridden husband, for instance, or cancer, or insanity, or a dozen other things from varied aspects of experience. In the religious experience the individual has the kind of lift and renewal that are good in and of themselves. In the experience itself evil seems remote and often unreal. Here I distinguish evil from sin as such. Perhaps this is due to the fact that the Christian brings into his religious experience as defined a belief and a persuasion that God is the final answer to all that there is, which includes evil itself. Nevertheless, the suffering is real and must be dealt with. It is in dealing with personal suffering and pain that the discipline of spirit may—and I emphasize the word may—guide one to the heart of religious experience. That it has this possibility is my only contention.

How is this done, when it is done? Suffering calls up all the resources of the individual. It tends to dominate his total horizon pushing all else aside. It becomes a great rallying point for energy. The individual fights for survival either in body, in spirit, or in soul. In the primary demand that is made upon the resources of spirit, the individual comes to a point of focus. He becomes centered first as a defense against the complete conquest by the suffering itself. Often this seems hardly possible. A simple case in point. I was ill for a few days with a bad case of tonsillitis. It involved a short period in the hospital. During the interval of illness, I tried to relieve my anguish by trying to recall how I felt when I did not have tonsillitis. I could scarcely remember. I was sure that if I could get a more adequate sweep of experience, the present disturbance could be absorbed or put in its place rather than taking over completely as it tended to do. The first spiritual problem created by suffering is the pain itself seen as an invasion of privacy, a violation of the orderliness of the personality and a denial of the good—thus undermining the validity of religious experience, perhaps. It is difficult to escape the demand to be preoccupied completely with one's suffering.

The second problem is the fact that the suffering seems a denial of the significance and worth of the individual. There is a quality of profound humiliation in suffering. This may be the basis for the intense hostility which is often inspired. I do not

know. At any rate the hostility is real and effective.
The hostility at first may be focused on the suffering itself. When this happens the suffering is
personified and becomes the emotional "whipping-
boy." Sometimes the individual uses the personifi-
cation of the suffering to tame it, to domesticate it,
and to make it a quiet companion.

To return to the aspect of hostility. Often the
hostility is focused upon persons who may directly
or indirectly be responsible in terms of cause and
effect for the suffering. But at long last the real
enemy is defined, God. The classic question finds
its way on the anguished lips, "Why did God do
this to me?" "Why am I punished?" "I do not
deserve it." And on and on it goes, repeating the
same theme. In my pain there is a miscarriage not
of justice merely but of human decency. Such acute
hostility cannot be resolved or drained off until
the individual faces God with his fact. Here I do
not mean accusing God in conversation with someone else about God and the why of the pain; I do
not mean hiding one's hostility under the fevered

words of someone else's outcry. No. None of these
will do. What I am thinking of is this: At last the
individual has to say directly to God in encounter
how he feels completely and thoroughly. This is
not easy because it is against the context of the
faith to "blow one's top" as it were to God about
God. It is a form of arrogance, of bumptiousness,
of blasphemy. Such behavior is to be irreverent.
Thus we repress our true feelings about the evil
with which we wrestle, and meanwhile our God
becomes a sleeping ghost among the stark hills of
our own barren wasteland.

What hostility may do is to serve as a guide
through the wilderness of our suffering until we
are brought to the door of the temple. When we
face God with our hostility, a kind of ultimate
suction takes place which empties us completely.
This is achieved in our confession to Him about
how we feel toward Him, toward life and perhaps
toward ourselves about our suffering. Out of our
struggle we may be given insight into the suffering
itself; we may be given quiet assurance, or we may

relax our intent into His Purpose, or we may turn it over to Him in quiet obedience. But this must be truly done.

I sat by a lady on the train one day who talked incessantly about nothing in particular. Suddenly she turned to me and asked, "Do you believe in prayer?" I replied very slowly, "Yes." "So do I," she said, quick as a flash. Continuing, she said, "Before I left home today, I took all of my troubles"—here she digressed for twenty minutes to fill in details—"made them into a neat bundle and handed them over to God; but before He could get the bundle unwrapped to take a look, I snatched them back again." It is this mood that must be guarded against in our suffering in relation to religious experience. It is particularly relevant because hostility tends to keep up the illusion of self-importance and pride. There are many people who would feel cheated if suddenly they were deprived of the ego definition that their suffering gives them.

The two spiritual problems created by suffering

—the personalizing of the problem of evil, and
hostility against God that is inspired—may become
handmaidens or guides into the very midst of the
encounter which is the heart of the religious
experience. Suffering requires an ultimate answer.
It must be dealt with in a manner which seems to
be at least provisionally conclusive. The logic of
the tragic fact is to lead the individual to whatever
are for him ultimate considerations. All of his
powers are focused on the issue involved in trying
to reduce his suffering to a manageable unit of
control, or to get rid of it. There is concentration
of the self already, and this is one of the prime
requisites for the religious experience. There is at
the heart of this concentration a search for an
ultimate fact capable of dealing with the rigors of
suffering. Hence the sufferer stands in immediate
candidacy for the very core of religious experience.
It should be pointed out that the attitude that I
have discussed calls attention to one of the live
options of the human spirit in dealing with suffering, which option has the possibility of "readying"

the spirit for religious experience. We come thus to the end of our examination of the inwardness of religion, and it is in order to turn now to a consideration of the outwardness of religion, or what is the result in the individual's personal behavior growing out of the religious experience itself?

THE OUTWARDNESS OF RELIGION

JESUS is dying. The sheer agony of the physical pain has reached its capacity. Beyond its present intensity it cannot go. Consciousness has slipped in and out of its socket. Nothing is left now but moments of awareness. It is at such a moment that the tempter whispers in tones filling all existence, "Prove it to them. Prove it. This is your final hour and your last chance." As if in perfect league with his invisible tormentor the swelling crowd picks up the echo of the terrible words, "Prove it. Prove it. Prove it. If you are the Son of God, come down from the cross and we will believe, believe, believe. Prove it. Believe." And thus he comes to the end with the last vestiges of exhaustion as he mutters, "Into Thy hands, into Thy hands."

Here we see dramatized the perennial dilemma
of religious experience. As has been pointed out
almost with weariness, the religious experience is
personal and private. It may be regarded as being
completely subjective. The fact is nothing against
the experience itself and in itself, but the individual must relate it to his total world of meaning.
The religious experience may remain unique, but
it must not be completely *"other"* as indeed it
cannot be. The real questions at issue here are, how
may a man know he is not being deceived? Is there
some guarantee against self-deception? Is there any
way by which he may know beyond doubt, and
therefore with verification, that what he experiences is authentic and genuine?

There are two problems inherent in these questions. One is the response to the demand for
rationality which is a part of the necessity of
adjustment to the environment. Life must make
sense. Experience must make sense. Whatever
seems to deny a fundamental structure of orderliness upon which rationality seems to depend

cannot be countenanced. In living his individual life a man must not seem to himself to be irrational, to be stupid. This demand is a part of the very integrity of life itself. This is a basis of the child's constant query, Why? Why? Why? The demand for order is the necessity of mind. Hence if the religious experience, as defined, is out of bounds for rationality, then it loses its personal accreditation or standing in the eyes of the individual experiencer. To have such an experience considered valid, the individual has to cut himself off from the rest of his fellows and in defense of such isolation must regard himself as more worthy and more worthful than all the rest. A person apart! Such self-regard makes for pride, arrogance, and all manner of illness of the spirit. Sometimes the defense takes the form of exclusiveness and separateness. There is such an element inherent in all religious experience. The problem seems insoluble and perhaps it is, I do not know.

If the religious experience is genuine and in it the individual has an assurance of communion

with God—this too has to fit into the facts of his
life as he knows them. The insistent fact is that
his life, as he himself knows it, does not merit
such fellowship. If he experiences it without merit,
then there is present, in the encounter, a gratuitous
element or grace. If the experience is characterized
by grace, then God is acting arbitrarily and from
within a totality that is not available to the individual himself. Hence God sees something in the
individual of which the individual himself is
scarcely aware. This marks the individual off from
his fellows and singles him out for special favor.
Unless the individual is able constantly to identify
himself with his fellows even in the presence of
God, he will vitiate his insights so that what is a
good in him at last becomes evil in its very uniqueness. But if he maintains his sense of identity with
his fellows, then what he is experiencing or experiences, all men everywhere stand in immediate or
indirect candidacy to experience, and a part of his
response to God is the shared knowledge of God's
availability to all. Once again we see how the fight

with pride becomes personal. The religious experience must belong *to* life and therefore be the
subject of understanding.

But there are two levels of understanding with
which we have to do in our effort to rationalize our
experiences of life. One is the grasp of the facts
themselves, the facts of our experiences. A study
of the facts cannot be undertaken until and unless
they are so regarded, i.e. regarded as facts. Always
our observation must be inclusive. One set of facts
of religious experience is the material that makes
up the personality of the individual. These include
not only personality structure but the individual's
responses to, and interpretation of, his total
heritage—in short, the total personality, his equipment, and his reaction to the raw materials of his
living. The observer who has the facts before him
may be able to interpret them, but here again his
interpretation has two crucial elements in it. One
is the fact of the integrity of the interpreter himself which must include his personality structure,
biases, fears, hopes, and so forth; the other is the

missing element in the facts not available to him as observer. That is, the meaning of the facts as seen by the person whose facts are under consideration.

We may illustrate our meaning here by reference to literary criticism. In reacting to the general tendency on the part of many young critics to gain if possible the right to pronounce definitive judgments on any field of literature on the basis of what we call creative criticism, T. S. Eliot says that he was

> inclined to take the extreme position that the only critics worth reading are the critics who practised well the art of which they wrote. But I had to stretch this frame to make important inclusions; and I have since been in search of a formula which could cover everything I wish to include, even if it includes more than I wanted. And the most important qualification which I have been able to find, which accounts for the peculiar importance of the criticism of practitioners, is that a critic must have a very highly developed sense of fact. This is by no means a

trifling or a frequent gift. . . . The sense of
fact is very slow to develop and its complete
development means perhaps the pinnacle of
civilization. For there are so many spheres of
facts to be mastered, and our uttermost sphere
of fact, of knowledge, of control will be ringed
with narcotic forces in the sphere beyond. . . .

There is a large part of critical writing which
consists in interpreting an author, a work. It
occasionally happens that one person obtains an
understanding of another or a creative writer,
which he can partially communicate and which
we feel to be true and illuminating. It is difficult
to confine the interpretation by external evidence. To anyone whose skill is in fact on this
level, there will be evidence enough, but who is
to prove his own skill? As for every success in
this type of writing, there are thousands of
impostors. Instead of insight, you get a fiction.
Your test is to apply again and again to the
original, with your view of the original to guide
you. But there is no one to guarantee your

competency, and once again we find ourselves in a dilemma.[1]

What this rather lengthy and somewhat involved quotation says with reference to literary criticism pertains in the whole matter under discussion at this point. Even at the level of the facts, it is very difficult to satisfy the total demand of objectivity. We are back to our first insistence that understanding of the facts of religious experience in an effort to establish their validity must take into account at least two levels of understanding. One level is the understanding that is derived from a study or examination of the facts themselves. The other level is the meaning of the facts as seen by the person experiencing them. How are they interpreted? Of course, such interpretation may be included in the facts themselves. But here again the observer stands outside of the interpretation. If with his experience, he stands somewhat inside the interpretation, then he is disqualified as a

[1] Selected Essays of T. S. Eliot, Harcourt Brace, 1932, pp. 31 ff.

judge because he cannot be objective. At every point he is bounded by his own identification. The meaning of the interpretation in the mind of the experiencer himself cannot be separated from the individual's needs, desires, hopes, fears, and so forth, which are his. Thus we are driven to some other basis of evaluation.

It may be here taken for granted that to the individual who has the religious experience, there is a logic and an integrity in the experience itself. And yet in the very nature of the case, he must test it. The experience must make a difference and a difference of such significance that the cause of the difference stands out clearly. But suppose it does not? What if never under any circumstances there is any difference? If the experience is persisted in, then the individual cannot ever escape the necessity for searching. This is one of the great paradoxes of religious experience. The validity of the religious experience does not ultimately rest upon the effect that it has in the world with which the individual has to do but, nevertheless, the individual is not ever relieved of the judgment of such a necessity.

We are now in a position to examine the question: Does religious experience, as defined, make a difference in the outward life of the individual, including in the outward life the very context in which such a person lives and functions?

In the first place the encounter with God in the religious experience gives to the individual a new focal point for his life. Ordinarily this is a matter of spiritual growth and development; for here is involved a central surrender of the self to God. It is in truest essence, commitment. It is this aspect of religious experience that is freighted with crises for the person. Even a cursory examination of the self reveals the nature of the problem presented by the demand for surrender. You have watched a little baby emerge slowly with a definition of himself. Perhaps the first step is the separation of the self from the not-self. The dawn of such discrimination in the mind of the child is a great revelation of the profound process of growth. The early form is found in the discovery of body distinction or body awarenesses as such. Then the emergence of another person, the mother, or the nurse as distinguished from himself. Slowly there appear various efforts at self-assertion, independence of the not-self. One of the great prophetic moments in the life of the child is when it is able to hold its own bottle, a definite manifestation of self-containment. Then in the crawling stages and in many ways prior to this stage, certain aspects of the immediate environment begin to develop their own character. The difference between softness and hardness, movable and immovable objects, and so forth, becomes apparent. Finally, as a result of unbearable pressure on the organism or in the organism, the body tries to stand—instinctively the child reaches out for support to anything at hand. What is in reach is put there by a kindly universe, and it may be something hanging down in front of him. He does not know that it is cloth. The cloth idea has not been a part of his experience. He does not know that it is a scarf and that it covers or decorates a table upon which rests a priceless vase for flowers. These things are beyond him. He seizes upon the suspended support and suddenly his whole world crashes; what is more important, his not-self, his mother, exposes him to further discomfort by some form of chastisement. Another day comes and he struggles upright alone. There, he is suspended between the ceiling and the floor with his little feet touching. Something is born deep within him and shouts as only he can hear, "I did it. I did it." Then without warning the floor rises up to meet him. I need not explore this further except to say that the struggle to achieve selfhood is rugged, tempestuous, and ruthless.

In the religious experience the individual is faced with the necessity of surrender which grows out of his response to God. Such a response is in terms of surrender. This surrender is accomplished in one of two ways. It may be a self-conscious yielding of the very center of one's being to God— the yielding of that of which the ego itself is but the shell, the façade, the protection, really. It is

Here is stated the problem of surrender: All your life we're taught to be independent; then comes God calling for commitment
68

what Douglas Steere has called the "nerve center
of consent." I do not know the anatomy of such
surrender nor indeed what precisely takes place.
In the Christian religion, for many, this is the point
at which Jesus Christ comes into thrilling significance. P. T. Forsyth writes:

> There is and can be nothing so certain to me
> as that which is involved in the most crucial and
> classic experience of my moral self, my con-
> scious, my real, surest me. . . . I must find my
> practical certainty in that which founds my
> moral life, and especially my new moral life.
> . . . The test of all philosophy is ethical convic-
> tion. That is where we touch reality—in moral
> action, and especially in that action of the moral
> nature which renews it in Christ. . . . What I
> have in Christ is not an impression but a life
> change; not an impression of personal influence
> which might evaporate, but a fact of central
> personal change. I do not merely feel changed.
> I am changed. Another becomes my moral life.
> He has done more than deeply influence me. He
> has possessed me. I am not His loyal subject,

but His absolute property. . . . He has given
me a new life, a new moral sense, a new consciousness of moral reality. There has been what
I can only call a new creation, using the
strongest word in my reach. . . . He has not
only impressed me as a vision might—even one
projected from my own interior—but He has
done a permanent work on me at my moral
center. He has made a moral change in me,
which for years and years has worked outward
from the very core of my moral self and subdued
everything else to its obedience. . . . My experience of Him is that of one who does a vital
revolutionary work in that moral region where
the last certainty lies. And in that region it is an
experience of a change so total that I could not
bring it to pass by any resource of my own. . . .
The great change was not a somersault I suc-
ceeded in turning, with some divine help; it was
the revolution effected in me and by Him.

Then after raising the question of the certainty
of the experience, he goes on to say:

There are hallucinations in religious experience but not here. They might be connected with
the affections, but not with the conscience at its
one-life-crisis. The experience has . . . an objective content, as is shown by the absolute rest
and decisive finality of its moral effects in my
life and conduct. . . . There is no rational
certainty by which this moral certainty could be
challenged; for there is no rational certainty
more sure, or so sure, and none that goes where
it goes, to the self-disposing centers of life.[2]

Here the surrender is at the core and is seen by
some Christians to be a surrender to Christ rather
than to God. In such a religious experience for
many the principals are the individual and Christ
who is here regarded as God. The central surrender of the center and the slow moral conquest
of the self, this is the struggle to carry the "transfer
of title" from the center to all the outlying districts

[2] P. T. Forsyth, *Hibbert Journal.* April, 1908, pp. 489–93
ff. Quoted by T. H. Hughes, *The Philosophic Basis of Mysticism.* Scribner, 1937, 189 ff.

of the self. The ups and downs of the Christian
experience find their real meaning at this point.
Falling and rising is the way, but there is a
center in the light of which judgment can always
be swift and decisive.

> Heir of the kingdom 'neath the skies,
> Often he falls, yet falls to rise,
> Struggling, bleeding, falling back,
> Holding still to the upward track,
> Playing his part in Creation's plan—
> God-like in image, this is man.

The other way by which the surrender is accomplished is in terms of particular situations or
events. Even over a long period of time the individual may make little surrenders, tiny surrenders,
apparently insignificant surrenders, morally un-
decisive surrenders, but always holding back the
ultimate, the final surrender. He finds himself torn
away from various attachments which may lodge
in his religious experience as things that must be
rooted out, or he may be willing to yield on all
the points which for him are not decisive; but deep

within himself he knows that he cannot hold out
indefinitely against the ultimate demand.

I fled Him, down the nights and down the days;
    I fled Him, down the arches of the years;
I fled Him, down the labyrinthine ways
    Of my own mind; and in the mist of tears
I hid from Him, and under running laughter.
                Up vistaed hopes I sped;
                And shot, precipitated,
Adown Titanic glooms of chasmèd fears,
    From those strong Feet that followed,
        followed after.[3]

What is the direct result of such surrender?
Does it work out from the center of one's life or
from the outer circle toward the center? Let us
examine this. The surrender of the self at its center
gives to the life a new basis for action. It provides
an integrated basis for action. Here at last the
individual has a core of purpose for his life and

[3] Francis Thompson, "The Hound of Heaven." Used by
permission of Burns, Oates & Washbourne, Ltd. and Sir
Francis Meynell.

for his living. There is a point at which for the individual the surrender of the self in religious experience gives to the life a purpose that extends beyond one's own private ends and personal risks. What happens to the individual is determined by what it is to which he surrenders. Also, there is a power in total surrender without regard to the worthfulness of the object to which the surrender is made. Too often this is forgotten or overlooked. There is inherent in the act of surrender the releasing of energies that are resident in that to which the surrender is made. This is true particularly when the object is regarded as being of supreme worth. This is the essence of the strange power and passion released in people who surrender to the state, for instance, and its embodiment, the dictator, as in fascism. Essential to what may be regarded as the dynamics of personal surrender is the releasing in the individual of new and great powers.

From whence come these powers? They are inherent in the individual, at least in part. Before surrender the individual spends enormous energies in scattered efforts, activities, and functions of various kinds. He is unable to bring to bear the resources of his life upon any single end. But when he surrenders and has now a new center which takes the form of a central demand, then his powers are pooled, are focused, and may be directed to achieve impossible ends. Our experience in recent years with fascism demonstrates this fully. Here is a reason in passing why in any immediate and open struggle with democracy, fascism for a while has the upper hand. Democracy is more scattered. It tends toward various levels of autonomies and certain kinds of general behavior. It is not until it is deeply challenged that its purpose takes on a metaphysical character and thus becomes a basis of integrated action. In such a struggle now the balance may shift to the side of democracy because the individual in a democracy may have a greater sense of universality and a more authentic sense of freedom. It is conceivable, however, and I think this is a part of the genius

of democracy, that there is something inherent in
the nature of the ideals for which it stands, or of
which it is symbolic, that is capable of inspiring
the same kind of devotion and sense of metaphysical purpose that is inherent in fascism. This is the
theory which in fact is rooted in certain over-all
assumptions with reference to the moral significance of democracy that are worthy of consideration but are apart from our purpose.

The dynamics inherent in the surrender become
immediately available to the life of the sur-
rendered person. His life is given back to him at
another level. Literally he loses his life and finds
it. In the surrender to God in the religious experience there is no loss of being but rather an irradiation of the self that makes it alive with "Godness"
and in various ways. There is awakened the desire
to be Godlike. This is no vague pious wish, no
moist-eyed sentimentality, but rather a robust
affirmation of the whole spirit of the man. This
is no casual interest in superficial goodness. It is
goodness at its profoundest depth. It is this kind

of goodness which must have been in the mind
of Jesus when someone addressed him as Good
Master and he said, "Why callest thou me good?
there is none good but God." To be good as God
is good becomes the overwhelming desire. This
means goodness not in contrast with evil, but
goodness in terms of wholeness, for lack of a better
term, of integration. Or again perhaps more
crucially in terms of creative synthesis. There must
be about God an "altogetherness" in which all
conflict is resolved and all tensions merge into a
single integration.

The point at which the desire to be good (which
in essence will be the achieving in living what he
has experienced in commitment) comes into conflict in the individual, is in the primacy of physical
existence itself. Much of the daily behavior of
mankind is informed by the desire to guarantee
and to perpetuate his own life. The strenuousness
of our effort is in behalf of protecting ourselves
from the impersonal operations of the world of
nature on the one hand and the impersonal opera-

tions of the social order on the other. The cultiva-
tion of the physical self has top priority. It is from
such a center that much daily motivation springs.
What happens then when there is a new center of
focus for the life? The answer to that, in part, is
this. At such a time as the new center becomes
operative, the individual relaxes his hold upon
himself as expressed in the self-regarding impulse.
A different kind of value is placed upon his physical existence. Death no longer appears as the great
fear or specter. The power of death over the individual life is broken. Death is no longer regarded
as the worst thing in the world, the great avenger,
but rather is it seen as it relates to the new individual, to be one of the servants of God to whom
the commitment is made. To lose this fear of death
and to regard it as a little thing is also a part of
the dynamics of commitment. There is no more
searching question than this: Under what circumstances would you yield your life with enthusiasm?
As long as a man holds his physical existence of
supreme importance, then he cannot make the

surrender inherent in any profound commitment.
But that to which he is committed must be of such
importance and of such supreme worth to him that
in exchange for this sharing, his life, his physical
existence is of no consequence. If a man holds his
life of supreme value above all values, then he
can always be controlled, enslaved, tyrannized,
mastered. All that is needed for his subservience
is the threatening of his physical existence. But if
the contrary is true, then to die may be gain. This
is the difference that the new center makes! The
simple story of the martyrs to the faith carries these
tidings. It must be remembered, however, that the
martyr is not to himself a martyr. He is positive,
not negative. I refer to this problem later.

Before passing on to the next phase of our discussion, one further observation must be made.
The willingness to yield one's physical life is an
intimation of what may be regarded as the character of the organized structure of the organism. The
fight for physical survival is one that is not a mere
matter of choice for the individual; it is rooted in

something vaster and much more inclusive of gross, as over against, refined purpose. Often when the curtain is pulled down on consciousness, as such, the battle for physical survival goes on without reference to what seems to be the self-conscious desire of the individual. Indeed one of the creative functions of coma is to turn all of the energies of the organism to the defeat of the enemy within the organism. It is small wonder that this determination which seems to be constitutional to all of life is formally elevated into a metaphysical principle called "the will to live." To be true to the commitment in the religious experience may cause the individual to go counter to the ends of physical life itself, and thus to be cut off from the strength that may be his from such support. Here we are faced with a deep and searching conflict. If there are values independent of the vitality of life as such, then are we not faced with a dualism which tears us from the meaning of totality itself? But even the function of elemental life is to sustain itself in ever higher differentiation, and the conflict between ends may be more apparent than real. The whole concept is brought into focus when the ethical mode of compassion enters into the struggle of life for survival. Whenever the weak are salvaged and nurtured, it may be that the perpetuation of the whole species is threatened; it may be that it is better for a whole species to disappear completely than that the moral life incipient in the first fleeting impulse to succour the helpless not be permitted to grow and unfold until goodness becomes "Godness." Of this I do not know.

The first expression of the outwardness of religion is the result on the life of the surrender of the self and its primary implications. The individual operates from a new center with all that is derived therefrom. The expression is the alteration of his private life growing out of a new value content. God has become the custodian of his conscience. This is of great significance. The center of loyalty allows meaning for the personality; the shift is from some primary social group loyalty, to

which the individual is related and which must not
be violated, to loyalty to the command of God. It
is a commonplace philosophy that our meaning as
persons is derived from our sense of belonging.
In our personal values, particularly at the point of
personal choices, the question which we ask when
confronted with the decision is apt to be, not what
do I really and truly want to do, or what is the
right thing to do; but rather, what bearing will my
action, whatever it is, have on my relationship with
those upon whose approval I depend for my own
rating, for my own self-estimate? In other words,
will my action cut the tie that binds me securely
to those whose life sustains my own, emotionally?
Conflict arises whenever the individual is faced
by a challenge to do that which is out of line with
what he conceives to be his duty to the group that
sustains him. When he violates the command of
the group, he is disturbed because his sense of
values has been thrown out of balance. Thus the
group becomes the custodian of his conscience and
his experience of right and wrong is involved in

group approval and disapproval. Mark you, I say his experience of right and wrong—that is, the content, but not the sense of values itself which is the channel of conscience.

When the individual's life comes under the influence of the God of his religious exposure, then the stage may be set for a soul-shaking conflict of loyalty. At last he must decide without regard to the bearing of the decision on his loyalty to the group. This decision calls for something much more coherent and intelligible than a mere feeling that this is what God demands of him. It is here that the concept of incarnation in the Christian faith takes on a practical significance. How does the individual know that his obedience is to God? Can he trust his interpretation of his finding, his residue of religious experience? The way is open now for some form of authority. The Christian finds the clue to his answer, yet even more than this, he finds the answers themselves, in the life and teachings of Jesus. Jesus becomes for such a view the *for instance* of the mind of God in reach of the tools of the individual. He *may* say, "I do not know what God requires. I'm not sure I can depend upon what seems to me the definite or definitive will of God. I am a creature of error, but I can know Jesus through the gospel and I share in the claim which is made for him that he is the word made flesh. He is in reach, and he can give me a tested series of formulae for the guidance of my own life because of the shared commitment which is ours. The study of his life thus becomes a necessity of my commitment."

Any personal behavior, then, that is out of harmony with his life and teaching becomes exposed to the swift judgment of what seems to me now to be his spirit. Slowly his mind becomes my mind, and then the amazing discovery that the mind that is more and more in me is the mind that was more and more in him. The mind that was in him becomes more and more clearly to me to be the mind that is God. All of this may be achieved without any necessity whatsoever of making a God out of Jesus.

I have referred earlier to the up-and-down quality of the struggle for religious character and goodness. The whole meaning begins now to unfold because I am concerned about the removing of the last barriers between the outer and the inner aspects of religious experience. It is not enough merely to have a new focus of orientation or to get a new will. These are crucial but not exhaustive. Certain other things must happen. In the sheer repetition of the religious experience, certain organic changes begin to take place in the very structure of the nervous system itself. This alteration results from the positive nervous response to the experience itself. Literally a new neurological pattern begins to emerge, which pattern slowly begins to supplant and then to undermine other established behavior patterns; thus, in time, giving to the total nervous system an altered neurological structure. But it must be held clearly in mind that the old pattern remains a threat and on occasion the new wires are jammed. We are accustomed to thinking in such terms when we consider the conversion experience. When we think about the meaning of the new life as defined in evangelical Christianity, it is along these lines that our thoughts run. I do not wish in my considerations here to cast any discredit upon the validity and miraculous character of transformation that may take place under such circumstances. But what I am insisting upon is that a regular experience of religion obtained over an indefinite time interval, having within that time interval numberless repetitions of the encounter—all of this will in time make certain structural changes in the behavior pattern of the nervous system itself. Thus the *body* becomes one of the evidences and consistent supports of the religious experience. This is very important and cannot be overemphasized.

The soundness of the concept or the analysis is doubly attested when we think of the meaning of the learning experience under any circumstances. It is this quality of remembering which the nervous system has that makes it possible for the individual to learn, thus making it unnecessary for the individual to do originally an act each time he performs the same act. The central question here is, can the repetition of the religious experience bring about such a reconditioning of the patterns of behavior within the organism and neurological structure as to make the organism itself expressive of the insight derived from the repeated experience? To me this seems perfectly reasonable. It would seem that as such a gradual structural change becomes operative, and is accompanied by a new or at least a different point of view; that is, a different conscious attitude toward life, toward experience, and toward people. It may be argued that the attitude comes first in a direct line from the religious experience and that such attitudes become the tutors of the nervous system and the reconditioning process. It seems to me, however, to be more accurately realistic to suggest that the sustained religious experience recurs on a curve of high frequency and of such constancy as to cause the mood and the quality of the religious experience to become the dominant, total mood of the individual. This is what happens structurally, I think, in personality that learns to live in the presence of God. Now once this is established, the personality becomes organized for hunting and ferreting out those aspects of the total behavior that work against the established mood. The guerrilla warfare goes on throughout life. Mind you, I'm not suggesting that such a mood roots out all that is evil in the nature, but it lays bare the evil to the light of the love and judgment of God as made manifest in the religious experience itself.

It is obvious that such consideration will make for an increasing honesty on the part of the individual. He knows that he jeopardizes his whole structure of religious meaning, and therefore security, if he deals dishonestly with the facts of his own life. In summing up this point, suffice it to say that the individual discovers that the contradictions in his own private life and experience are not in and of themselves ultimate contradictions, but that he is constantly exposed to a sense of creative synthesis in his religious experience that defines his assignment with the details of his day-by-day living.

With reference to how such a person relates to his fellows, it is sufficient to say that no man can be independent of his fellows. He must relate to them in some way that is meaningful to him. The discussion of this aspect of our consideration is reserved for our final chapter.

The question at issue *here* is the kind of personal context out of which the individual relates to his fellows. There are two basic ways by which the individual interprets himself. One is in the light of the facts of his life as seen by him. Each individual has the inside track on his fact or his facts. But his vision may be blinded by another consideration, namely, the image of himself which he has. This image then is the other way by which he interprets himself. We are apt to be more influenced by the image which we have of ourselves than by the fact of ourselves. The image provides for a much more

permissive interpretation. We can hide it success-
fully from our fellows for a long time perhaps.
Their only encounter with it is in the shadow
which it casts on our behavior, but even here they
may be guessing and the individual exposed to all
the vulnerability of any other kind of projection.
Yes, we may hide the image and never disclose
it. The facts of ourselves are more directly available to us but only partially available to others. My
personal context out of which I relate to my
fellows or out of which I manifest the result in
personal terms of my religious experience is made
up of these two elements—the facts concerning
myself and the image of myself.

It is interesting to point out, before pursuing
this further, that each person with whom I am
related has also the two elements in his estimate
or interpretation of me, the facts as he sees them
concerning me and the image that he has of me as
a person. Very often he is guided by the image
which he has of me rather than by the fact or any
combination of these two. It is a very searching

question. What is the extent to which the individual is able to integrate his sense of fact, in
regard to other people or another person, with his
sense of image, in regard to other people or
another person? One of the results of a healthy
personality is the ability so to understand both the
image and the facts that they become more and
more integrated and the individual becomes in-
creasingly whole. But this requires a special kind
of honesty, a special kind of integrity. If it is true,
as we are insisting, that in the religious experience
the individual sees himself as he is and as God sees
him and makes an honest surrender, then such
an experience would give to the individual an
integrity of appraisal with reference to the facts
of his own life and the pretensions which are
often present in the image. Thus the externalizing
of my inner religious experience becomes my
response to the God of my religious experience.
It is in my response formally that I reveal utterly
the meaning of this life. But in order to examine
the full significance of what is meant here, we

must make a total digression in our next chapter, by examining what is the ground for this inner need for love that finds its flowering in the most illuminating aspect of religious experience; namely, that the individual has a sense of being completely and thoroughly understood and of being dealt with at a point in him that is beyond good and evil. This means that the individual becomes conscious that he is the recipient of the love of God.

III THE INNER NEED FOR LOVE

an excellent cl

DESPITE the fact that each person is in some degree mindful of the deep personal need which he has for love, the recognition of the fact has only recently become a part of the total understanding and study of personality. For reasons not far to seek we have been embarrassed by the admission of the fact itself and unwilling to face the implications of such a fact for our own experience and for the meaning of our lives. This reservation is a part of the general attitude toward feelings to which I referred in a passing sentence at the beginning of the discussion.

In the *Science Newsletter* for January 2, 1954, there is a very interesting article in the section on animal psychology called "Gentled Baby Rats

92

Stand Stress Better." The article begins by saying that babies who get TLC—tender loving care—probably will be better able to stand stress and will be less likely to develop heart trouble, high blood pressure, and stomach ulcers when they grow up than those babies who are not so gently handled. A study made with baby rats seemed to indicate this. Such a study was reported by Dr. Otto Winenger of the University of Toronto at the recent meeting of the American Association for the Advancement of Science held in the city of Boston. The method of gentling was very simple. The scientist held the rat in his hand close to his chest and stroked its back from the head to the base of the tail. This operation was repeated many times. It developed that the gentled rats gained more weight than the others; their bones grew more, and they were less fearful in strange situations. When put under severe stresses, including being held without food or water for forty-eight hours, the gentled animals showed less tendency to hardening of the blood vessels, and stomach

avoit panic

and intestinal disorders than the rats that were not gentled. The doctor in his report suggested that the relative immunity of the gentled animals to stress damage was due probably to a decrease of ACTH output from the pituitary glands with less release of hormones from the adrenal glands. The not-gentled rats showed nervous adrenal glands following stress.

The concept of TLC is very crucial for the development of personality as well. This has been demonstrated by various people under varying circumstances, particularly by those people who work with children. In the fact-finding report of the Midcentury White House Conference on Children and Youth, there is a very discriminating discussion on the meaning of personality and a descriptive analysis of the course of healthy personality development. A definition of personality is suggested as follows:

> The thinking, feeling, acting, human being, who, for the most part, conceives of himself as an individual separate from other individuals

and objects—this human being does not *have* a
personality; he *is* a personality.[1]

As a personality the human being has needs that
cannot be separated from his needs as a human
creature. The report continues to say:

> It has been well established that loving care
> is essential for the well-being of children. . . .
> This principle regarding the importance of lov-
> ing care for the well-being of children has
> already had revolutionary consequences where
> it has been wisely applied; for instance, in
> certain institutions for children.[2]

There is another section under the heading, "The
Importance of Love and Guidance." The report
has this to say:

> That children need love that is expressed in
> solicitous care for their welfare is another
> dictum of modern psychology that is well con-

[1] *A Healthy Personality for Every Child*, Midcentury White
House Conference on Children and Youth, 1951, p. 3.
[2] *Ibid.*, p. 5.

firmed by numerous studies. What is often overlooked is that nearly all parents, even the most
"rejecting," have affection for their children.
. . . Child guidance workers find that even
those parents and children who are most
embroiled in expressing hostility are likely to
have love for each other that is hidden under
their anger.[3]

Some of the research that has been going on in
this connection reveals very startling facts. In a
study called *War and Children* Anna Freud and
Dorothy Burmingham report on their observa-
tions in the care of children who had to be
separated from parents during the exigencies of
war. In the introduction to the study, the authors
state that it has already been generally recognized
that the lack of essential food vitamins and so
forth in early childhood will cause lasting bodily
malformations in later years, even if harmful conse-
quences are not immediately apparent. It is not
generally recognized that the same is true for the

[3] *Ibid.*, pp. 39 ff.

mental development of the child. When certain essential needs are not fulfilled, lasting psychological malformations will be the consequence. These essential elements are "the need for personal attention, for emotional stability, and for permanency of educational influence." These first two are fundamental to the topic of our present discussion, "The Inner Need for Love." The study concludes with the observation:

> The emotional relations of the small child to his parents are of importance to his development in two main respects. One is that this childish love is the pattern for all later love relationships. The ability to love, like other human faculties, has to be learned and practiced. Whenever, through the absence of or interruption of personal ties, this opportunity is missing in childhood, all later relationships will develop weakly and will remain shallow.[4]

What may be regarded as the negative aspects

[4] *War and Children*, International University Press, 1944, 190.

of the problem are also being studied very care-
fully in many quarters. Dr. John Bowlby in his
monograph called "Maternal Care and Mental
Health" goes into some detail in his analysis of the
adverse effects of what is called maternal depriva-
tion. One of the most widely known studies,
however, is by Dr. Rene Spitz under the title
*Hospitalism, an Inquiry into the Genesis of Psy-
chiatric Conditions in Early Childhood.* I refer
basically to Volume I. The general, though
limited, conclusions are very far-reaching. Those
children under two years old who were deprived
of a mother substitute show increased susceptibility
to infection, in spite of high hygienic and nutri-
tional standards of the institutions in which they
are placed. Children under three months show no
demonstrable impairment, but those in hospitals
for more than eight months in the first year show
such severe psychiatric disturbances that they cannot even be tested. Further, after three years
changes are irreversible. Finally, those hospitalized
during the first year have no hope at all. Those in

the second and third year can be partially cor-
rected. It is interesting to point out the causes as
summarized by Dr. Spitz. There are two basic
causes. First, the lack of stimulation. He says that
best equipped and most hygienic institutions are
worse because they sterilize not only the germs but
the child's personality. The most destitute of
homes offers more stimulation than a hospital
ward. Second, the presence or absence of the
mother. Those with the mother had better results
than those who had only trained nurses. Presence
of the mother could compensate for numerous
shortcomings in other areas.

I was discussing this whole problem with a
medical friend who told me that very often when
he was in pediatric service, the chief of the service
would prescribe TLC for certain children who
were showing obvious signs of withdrawal and
were losing their interest in their surroundings.
We were discussing this at dinner. Sitting near us
was a clergyman of mutual acquaintance. He
listened with rapt attention. After the doctor had

finished speaking, the minister told us of his younger son who had to be hospitalized when he was less than a year old. The battle for life was long and arduous. The malady was a baffling one. Certain degenerative processes in bodily tissue were taking place and could not be arrested. The child would take no food, had no interest in his surroundings, and was more and more listless and withdrawn. As a last desperate effort to save the child's life, the chief of the service gave an order that two nurses were to spell each other around the clock in making it their first responsibility to take the baby up, cuddling and loving him in their arms for long and stated intervals. After several days it seems that something deep within the child began to stir, to respond. There was a gradual interest in food and in the surroundings, and in time the degenerative process was halted. The child began the long road back to health. Now, says his father, he is a very active and vigorous high school athlete.

It seems clear from these studies and even from

casual observation that the need for love is so
related to the structure of the personality that
when this need is not met, the personality is
stunted and pushed or twisted out of shape. Here
we are not dealing with some luxury item for
personality but rather with an utter necessity. If
such a need is so basic in the life of the child, then
its fulfillment must not be left merely to the whim
and mood of the parent. That is to say, nature
must of necessity be wise enough to know already
what we are slowly discovering. There must be
some provision made for this in the personality
of the mother at a point that is more profound
than that which is merely voluntary or volitional.
Here it is an obvious need in the very nature of
the child. Something in the nature of being a
mother must be present to deal with that need.
This something is mother love. It seems that this
quality is indigenous in the female structure.

In searching for this element in the structure of
the mother, I came upon a most arresting study
called *The Soul of the White Ant* by Eugene

Marais. The author offers a very significant explanation for the existence of mother love among
lower animals, which seems to guarantee the
response on the part of the mother to the need so
central in the life of the offspring. In discussing
pain and travail in nature, he finds that all animals
possess some mechanism for feeling pain, and the
pain always acts as a safeguard against death. Pain
is the great danger signal. It is the red light. If
animals could feel no pain, they would not be able
to survive. They would not be conscious of many
things in their environment that threaten and
ultimately destroy, if they go unnoticed, and if
the organism does not seek to protect itself. This
is true of all pain except the pain of birth. The
key to mother love, suggests Mr. Marais, is birth
pain. Where birth pain is absent, there is abso-
lutely no mother love exercised with reference to
the offspring. He goes on to say:

> [The instances] where pain is negligible,
> mother love and care are feeble. Where pain is
> absent, there is absolutely no mother love. Dur-

ing a period of ten years' observation, I found
no single exception to this rule. Some naturalist
once suggested that the function of birth pain
was to draw the attention of the mother to the
young one. This is not so. There is no such thing
as 'drawing attention' in the instinctive soul.
The unlocking of the mother love complex
through pain is beyond consciousness, beyond
the knowledge of the mother, and has nothing
to do with drawing her attention to her offspring.[5]

The author conducted a series of experiments
with a herd of sixty half-wild South African Kaffir
bucks. He states categorically that during the
previous fifteen years there had been no single case
of the mother refusing her young under normal
circumstances. Now what results did he find?
First, there were six cases of birth during full
anesthesia of the mother induced by chloroform
ether. Unconsciousness lasted about twenty-five
minutes after delivery. In each case the mother

[5] *The Soul of the White Ant,* Dodd, Mead, 1937, 111.

refused to accept the lamb by her own volition. Second, there were four cases of birth during paralysis when consciousness and feeling were only partially paralyzed. In each case the mother was in great doubt for more than an hour as to the acceptance of the lamb. After this period, three accepted, one rejected. Further tests to check whether or not the refusals were due to problems created for the mother by the introduction of anesthesia were negative. In six cases the mother was put under chloroform anesthesia immediately after delivery was complete, but before she had seen her lamb. Unconsciousness lasted a half hour. In each case the mother accepted the lamb after she became conscious. The over-all conclusion is reached as far as animals are concerned that without pain there can be no mother love in nature. Such pain has to be experienced psychologically. It is not sufficient merely to experience it physiologically. The author concludes:

The degeneration of the sexual sense is responsible for the greatest part of human suffering. Yet one part of sex, mother love, gave a twist to man's psychological development which was largely responsible for his domination of the earth.[6]

The analogy may seem farfetched because if it is true, as the author claims, it applies to so-called lower animals. Mother love may not have its immediate roots in organic pain as far as human beings are concerned. The effort here is to establish what seems to be what was originally the organic basis for this response on the part of the human mother to the human baby. Social customs and social behavior patterns perpetuated by memory tutoring may be regarded as being more directly responsible for the presence of mother love as the norm among human beings and their offsprings.

To summarize, the need for love is an essential element in the structure of personality. It is responsible for the establishing of a pattern of response to other human beings that makes possible all

[6] *Ibid.,* p. 114.

forms of community and of relatedness between
human beings in society.

It is in order then to examine the form that this
need takes at the adult level. Here the need is for
being understood, for being accepted in terms of
one's intrinsic worth rather than merely for what
one does or does not. It is a hunger for counting
in solely for one's self, rather than because of what
one has to contribute or to share, or because of
one's status, one's parents, one's background, or
any of the other trappings by which personality
seeks on various occasions to express itself. There
is no feeling quite comparable to the adult feeling
that someone cares for you as *you* without any
extras involved. Each person longs for the kind
of relationship with others in which it is no longer
necessary to pretend in any sense whatsoever. In
other words there is the deep need to be dealt with
in some sense that is total, that is all-inclusive, that
is completely complete.

One of the ways by which this expresses itself
in adult life is in the need to be needed. There is

nothing more searching in its exhilaration than
the experience of meeting the need in another
person at the point that the need is most acutely
felt. This is to count in a way that is not conditioned. However, it is very significant to realize
the influence that this need has had upon human
history and particularly upon the development of
certain aspects of Christianity.

It is the recognition of this deep need in personality that may be *one* of the elements in the significance which is attached to the Virgin Mary in
Catholicism, and perhaps even in contemporary
Catholicism. It is aside from my purpose to undertake any evaluation of Mariolatry as such, but it
is crucial to our discussion to examine the significance of the development in the religion which
was completely captured by a masculine trinity.
The deep need for being understood beyond all
limitations of life, circumstances, and character
stands out in boldest relief here. The literature of
that period abounds in illustrations of the part the
Virgin played in giving to the ordinary man and

woman, as well as the high and mighty, a sense of worth which was independent of any of their recommendations or deserts.

A classic illustration is that of the tumbler or foot acrobat who, out of disgust with the world, joined the monastery at Clairvaux. He was an ignorant man as well as unlettered, and therefore found it impossible to join in the regular services in the chapel.

> He could not say his prayers by rote;
> Not "Pater Noster"; not a note;
> Not "Ave Mary," nor the creed;
> Nothing to help his soul in need.

It is not difficult to understand the sense of futility and worthlessness that pressed in upon him. He felt that he did not count. He had no authentic sense of belonging. The constant fear that he would be dismissed haunted his days and made miserable his sleep. One day when the bells were calling to mass, he hid in the crypt and talked his problem through with the Virgin. He decided:

At least I'll do what I've been taught!
At least I'll serve in my own way
God's Mother in her church today.
The others serve to pray and sing.
I will serve to leap and spring.

Then he made himself ready, took off his gown,
but covered himself with a jacket soft and thin.
When he was ready, he offered this prayer:

"Lady!" says he, "to your care
I commit my soul and frame.
Gentle Virgin, gentle dame,
Do not despise what I shall do,
For I ask only to please you,
To serve you like an honest man,
So help me God, the best I can.
I cannot chant, nor can I read,
But I can show you here instead,
All my best tricks to make you laugh, . . .
Lady, who never yet could blame
Those who serve you well and true,
All that I am, I am for you."

Then he did his act until he fell unconscious on the altar steps. Every day he did this, giving to the Virgin a private showing of what he knew best how to do. Finally his absence was noted by one of the monks. He was spied on and reported to the Abbot. The Abbot decided to watch for himself. He observed the tumbler lying in an unconscious state at the foot of the altar. Then as he watched, the Virgin herself stepped down, along with her angels and archangels, all to give him solace and comfort.

> And the lady, gentle, true,
> Holds in her hand a towel new;
> Fans him with her hand divine
> Where he lies before the shrine.
> The kind lady, full of grace,
> Fans his neck, his breast, his face!
> Fans him herself to give him air!
> Labours, herself, to help him there!
> The lady gives herself to it;
> The poor man takes no heed of it;

> For he knows not and cannot see
> That he has such fair company.[7]

Here we have depicted in simple lines the way in which the Virgin in the thought of the period speaks to the deepest needs of the human spirit—to be completely and thoroughly understood. Henry Adams describes the significance of the Queen of Heaven in unforgettable prose.

There is heaven! And Mary looks down from it, into her church, where she sees us on our knees, and knows each one of us by name. There she actually is—not in symbol or in fancy, but in person, descending on her errands of mercy and listening to each one of us, as her miracles prove; or satisfying our prayers merely by her presence which calms our excitement as that of a mother calms her child. She is there as Queen . . . and her power is such that to her the difference between us earthly beings is nothing. Her quiet, masculine strength enchants us most. . . . The

[7] Henry Adams, *Mont-Saint-Michel and Chartres,* Houghton, 1936, 281 ff.

Bishop himself is not quite at his ease in her presence; but to peasants, and beggars, and people in trouble this sense of her power and calm is better than active sympathy. People who suffer beyond the formulas of expression—who are crushed into silence, and beyond pain—want no display of emotion—no bleeding heart—no weeping at the foot of the cross—no hysterics —no phrases! They want to see God and to know that He is watching over His own. How many women are there, in this mass of thirteenth century suppliants, who have lost children? Probably nearly all, for the death rate is very high in the conditions of medieval life. There are thousands of such women here, for it is precisely this class who come most; and probably every one of them has looked up to Mary in her great window and has felt actual certainty, as though she saw with her own eyes—there, in heaven, while she looked—her own lost baby playing with the Christ-Child at the Virgin's knee, as much at home as the saints and much more at home than the kings. Before rising from her knees, every one of these women will have bent down and kissed the stone pavement in gratitude for Mary's mercy. The earth, she says, is a sorry place, and the best of it is bad enough. . . . But there above is Mary in heaven who sees and hears me as I see her, and who keeps my little boy till I come; so I can wait with patience more or less! Saints and prophets and martyrs are all very well, and Christ is very sublime and just, but Mary *knows!* [8]

In my opinion this same basic need is present in certain aspects of Protestantism. When worship becomes too formal and disembodied, there is a demand for humanizing it. The literature of the Gospel hymn reveals in striking manner the creative necessity for the average Protestant Christian to make his God and his Christ directly available to his spirit as one who comforts, who wipes the tear from the eye, who is the personal friend and daily companion. It is not an overstatement to

[8] *Ibid.,* pp. 195 ff.

suggest that the birth of Buddhism as a religion
of compassion grew out of a necessity deep within
the need of the devout Hindu when the ethical
concept of reverence for life became more and
more a metaphysical principle.

We come now to the baring of the fact of the
need for love on the religious experience as we are
thinking of it in this series. It was pointed out in
our first chapter that one demand that is made
upon religious experience is that it be private,
personal, individual, and in some very important
sense, unique. It is never sufficient for the individual to have a clue merely to ultimate significance in general, but there must be provided in the
religious experience a sense of the ultimate worth
of the individual himself as a private person. This
demand finds expression in the concept of the
infinite worth of the individual in the sight of
God.

It is in connection with this second demand that
the significance of the inner need for love finds its
ultimate fulfillment and its final triumph. There

is a direct continuity between the need to be loved,
to be deeply cared for, and the heart, the very pulse
beat of the individual's experience of God in the
religious encounter. Here the individual is laid
bare, stripped of all façade—what I am in and of
myself is finally dealt with. The person has a sense
of being touched at his deepest center, at his very
core, and all other experiences of love are but
intimations of this great experience. All other
experiences of love at the other levels are what
may be regarded as "readying" experiences for the
great and tremendous experience which is the significant element in the religious experience itself.
This is the essence of the meaning of the love of
God. In the presence of God, at last, a man is
relieved of all necessity for pretending. He can
stand clean in the sense of being undisguised and
utterly without shame. This does not mean that
limitations are overlooked, that sins are no longer
sins, but it does mean that anything less than the
very core of one's being is not quite relevant. To
be touched *there* is to be placed in a position to

have one's life thoroughly examined, thoroughly explored, but from the center, the ultimate point of reference within the individual. There is nothing that cannot be dealt with here. There is nothing that cannot be handled or encompassed from this point of leverage. There is nothing that cannot be understood, placed in this perspective of the event and the logic of one's own life. Here a man is at the headwaters of his very being. What happens here truly happens. This is the very citadel itself. The religious experience carries with it the judgment that this encounter with God is completely exhaustive and all-comprehending. Out of this experience the Psalmist speaks,

> O Lord, thou hast searched me, and known me. Thou knowest my downsitting and my uprising, Thou understandest my thought afar off. . . . For there is not a word in my tongue, but, lo, O Lord, thou knowest it altogether. Thou hast beset me behind and before, and laid thine hand upon me. Such knowledge is too wonderful for me; it is high, I cannot attain unto it.

In the early part of our discussions, we were reminded that the first love of the child is very important in the child's education. That is, this first response of the child to TLC has far-reaching results for the child's development. To repeat the suggestion merely as a reminder here, education demands from the child continuous sacrifices. The child has to give up its primitive habits, to become clean, to lessen his aggressions, and so forth. He is ready to pay this price if he gets his parents' love in return. If such love is not available, education either has to threaten or to drill or to bribe—all methods unsatisfactory in their results.

Here we are faced with the same basic situation. Growth in Godlikeness, spiritual maturity, demands continuous sacrifices on the part of the individual. In the religious experience certain demands are made upon the individual. Much of this was referred to in the previous chapter.

Let us explore it further and from another position. In order to have the deep need for love met in the religious experience, the individual has to

give up something. What? He must give up those
things which put him out of communication with
God—those things which make it impossible for
him to meet God in the trysting place. This is
essential to his development in spiritual awareness.

It is for this reason that there is inevitably associated with religious experience some aspect of
crisis. There is the tension created by the response
to grow, to be, and to become more Godlike, and
the terrible pull to remain as one is. All of the
things in one's life that meet secondary needs must
be constantly scrutinized in the light of the
demands of the experience itself. If there is in me,
for instance, an attitude, the presence of which fills
me with shame in God's presence, something must
be done about it. There is no substitute for a
thoroughgoing honesty in facing it. Here I cannot
run the risk of even a seeming deception. I must
admit all down to the final quiver of my own spirit.
The insight of Jesus is almost terrifying in its
clarity here. He says, "If thy hand or thy foot
offend thee, cut them off. . . . If thine eye offend

thee, pluck it out." "No man can serve two masters," he continues in another place. As the religious experience grows in meaning and in frequency until its mood begins to seep through all the levels of one's awareness, one becomes more and more sensitized to the things that blur its beauty and holiness. It is not so much that God requires it as it is the fact that the individual sees that this, or that, or the other thing blurs his vision.

Some years ago I heard Miriam Slade tell the story of her early days as a member of Gandhi's Ashram in India. When she journeyed to India to become a part of the group around Gandhi, she was sure that before she left home she had gotten rid of all attachments to possessions and all of her possessions. She was down to what she was sure of as being the basic minimum. But for several months she sent more and more parcels back to England. As she moved more deeply into belong-ing, she felt that she had to give up more and more. The result was that when I saw her several years after, in America, she had traveled from India to

England and to America and with her were all of
her earthly goods: a winter coat; a Kodda cloth
sari, two of them; a small cotton bag that had a few
personal articles in it; and on her feet the sandals
made from an animal that died a natural death.
This represented her worldly possessions. The
operation of the principle of sacrifice about which
I am thinking is illustrated here. The demands that
are inherent in the situation become the determin-
ing factors.

You may recall that during the war General
Doolittle and a crew in his airplane were flying
across the Pacific. They ran into difficulties and
they felt that the only way by which they could
guarantee arriving at an island or some place
where they could land with some measure of safety
was to reduce the total load of the ship. They had
to make hard choices. They threw overboard all
of the extra gasoline which they carried and then
one by one various things were dumped overboard,
the purpose of which was to make the plane lighter
and lighter so as to guarantee the chances of sur-

vival, until, at last, even the mailbags that had
precious documents for the government had to be
thrown over in one final dramatic effort to survive.
This illustrates in still another way the basic
principle which is explicit in the religious experience. In the presence of God all of the things that
stand between me and the total exposure of myself
to His love must be systematically or radically
gotten rid of. Here again, I repeat that it is not due
merely to a demand which God makes of me, but
it is rather due to a recognition of the fact that
there are those qualities of personality, those
attachments to things, those desires that succeed
in blurring the vision and limiting the sense which
I must have of being totally and completely
encompassed by the love of God. There is a long
straight line from the stirring in the heart of the
child in response to the love of the mother to the
stirring at the core of one's being in response to
the love of God. This is the journey. This is the
meaning. This is the logic of the deep inner need
that every individual has for love and which

expresses itself ultimately in the matured religious experience when one comes into the full knowledge of the meaning of the lines of Augustine, "Thou hast made us for thyself and our souls are restless till they find their rest in thee."

The important thing is not that I must sacrifice against my will. It is that the experience of God in religious experience creates in me the desire *to* desire to give up more and more that which impedes my growth and my development in the knowledge and the love of God. The Christian witness through the ages bears this out and not only the Christian witness. No man can look on God's face and remain as he was. The term "sacrifice" is perhaps not an accurate one. It is a term used by the observer but never used by the person in the encounter. Central to the growth of the personality in God is the demand that the experience makes for giving up or sacrifice.

This observation or insight may throw a flood of light on the whole psychology of martyrdom, particularly in the Christian religious experience.

The man who becomes a martyr is not of necessity
one who is suffering from some kind of internal
emotional disturbance. It may not be the manifestation of an abnormal personality that is at work
here, but rather the martyr may be regarded as a
man who arrives at a point in his experience of
God in which the estimate that he places upon his
physical existence becomes secondary. Therefore,
he is faced with a decision which seems to him to
turn on whether or not on behalf of the truth that
is in him, truth derived from experience of the love
of God in his life, he is willing to sacrifice even
life itself. He must make a choice. He will choose
rather to do the thing that is to him the maximum
exposure to the love and therefore to the approval
of God, rather than the thing that will save his
own skin. Perhaps this is what Jesus meant when
he raised the question as to what a man would give
in exchange for his life. The profoundest disclosure in the religious experience is the awareness
that the individual is not alone. What he discovers
as being true and valid for himself must at last

be a universal experience, or else it ultimately loses all of its personal significance. His experience is personal, private, but in no sense exclusive. All of the vision of God and holiness which he experiences, he must achieve in the context of the social situation by which his day-by-day life is defined. What is disclosed in his religious experience he must define in community. That which God shareth with him, he must inspire his fellows to seek for themselves. He is dedicated therefore to the removing of all barriers which block or frustrate this possibility in the world. He is under judgment to make a highway for the Lord in the hearts and in the market place of his fellows. Through his living men must find it a reasonable thing to trust Him and to trust one another and therefore to be brought nearer to the great sacramental moment when they too are exposed to the love of God at a point in them beyond the evil and the good. What does this mean in terms of the social situation in which we find ourselves and particularly what does it say concerning the witness of the church?

IV   THE OUTER NECESSITY FOR LOVE

WE come now to the summary of our reflections. We have discussed the inward and the outward aspects of religion considered from within the narrow boundaries of personal life and experience. We have located one of the authentic grounds of religious experience in the need of the human spirit for love and the logic of the fulfillment of that need in the religious experience of the love of God. It is in order to raise the question as to the bearing of this kind of religious experience upon the social and institutional context in which individuals move and have their being. Does the individual coming out of such a religious experience as defined make any impact on the cultural pattern which is his, and can the cultural pattern be so operated upon that it reflects the society in a manner that is favorable to the kind of religious experience discussed?

If it is true that the two principals of the religious experience are God and the individual, then the religious experience is both individual and God-centered. Any shift in the cultural pattern which would make the cultural pattern itself more individual-centered or personality-centered, would enhance the possibility of the meaning of life for the individual.

Dr. James Plant in his illuminating study, *"Personality and the Cultural Pattern,"* discusses what he calls certain "centering-points" in terms of which a cultural pattern can be understood. In this phase of my discussion I am following his analysis. The world has witnessed a series of cultural patterns in the course of the development of man on this planet. There is, for instance, the God-centered culture. In such development the significance of personality is measured in terms of the personality's service and usefulness to God. The

contribution of such a culture to its community
is in terms of the bearing of the experience of the
individual upon the meaning of his service to God.
The social institutions in such a culture are given
the benediction of God and the efficacy of their
existence turns on the degree to which they serve
this God. In reality the individual counts very
little except as he is actively involved in the service
to God.

Another type is the family-centered culture. The
point of significance is the furtherance and the
continuance of the family as a social institution.
The relevancy of the individual is defined in terms
of the way in which the individual fits into the
need of the family. If he is contributing to the
permanence of the family, he counts. If he is outside of a family constellation due to factors or
forces that are out of his control, he has no way by
which the significance of living can be established
for him. He is lost.

Then there is the state-centered culture. The
significance and the stability of the individual are

conditioned by the degree to which he contributes
to the centrality of the state. In this kind of society,
the state defines the meaning of individual status,
worth, and meaning. Such a culture pattern tends
to be very dynamic and energizes every expression
of social process. Out of it comes the cult of the
leader as the symbol of the state.

Then there is the profit-centered culture. The
significance of the individual is defined in terms
of the relevancy of his contribution to the economic
order and its stability. Even values are defined in
terms of economic units or economic goods. I was
impressed when I read a casualty insurance policy
in which there is a table giving a list of injuries
and their corresponding compensation guarantees
in terms of dollars. For instance, a knee injury,
fifty dollars; loss of one eye, one thousand dollars,
and so forth. In such a society a certain number of
dollars will be paid for a broken heart. The whole
category of damages to personality, to feelings, to
reputations, intangible things, is measured in
money equivalents. In all of these "centering points"

for the culture, there is an obvious recognition of
the fact that they represent an effort to meet certain
of the basic needs of the individual; to give to the
individual a sense of belonging, of relatedness, of
significance. These centers are *symbols of life* but
soon become involved in the simple human tendency of giving life itself to what are essentially
symbols of life. The moment this happens, the
centering point takes on certain characteristics
which Plant calls "dynamic factors." These characteristics express themselves in terms of controls, in
terms of patterns of conservative action, and
demands for service to them, rather than the giving
of service to the individual. In an effort to stabilize
itself the cultural pattern tends to lose sight of the
individual needs for which it was created, and
instead to make the individual the tool of the
pattern.

The logic of the kind of religious experience
that we have been describing points toward an
individual-centered culture pattern. If in something as significant as the religious experience the

individual personality is the crucial point of reference, not because of who the individual is, or what
the individual is, or the shape of his head, or the
color of his eyebrows, then it follows that a society
that is personality-centered would provide a
climate predisposed to religious experience and
all that it indicates for the enrichment and meaning of life.

The first and most immediate obligation of the
person whose life is fed by such religious experiences is to seek to apply the insights derived to the
problems of his daily life. What demands must
he make upon himself on behalf of his religious
experience? Here the individual is not merely
faced with matters of personal piety, but he is
confronted with the necessity for giving expression
to his life as a responsible member of his society.
All of his living in the midst of his fellows
becomes in a sense his religious vocation.

Precisely what does this mean? In the first place,
he must make his choice of work, of vocation in a
more restricted sense, in the light of his religious

commitment. For instance, it will not be enough
for him merely to be a well-trained doctor, or
lawyer, or teacher. His professional training becomes a part of his total commitment to God,
growing out of his religious experience. More and
more his life *totally* belongs to the God of his
dedication. The tools, the skills, the training, the
resources of every kind which are his must be at
the disposal of the commitment derived from his
religious experience. The dichotomy that exists
between his professional life and his private life,
between his formal life and his informal life,
between his inner life and his outer life, must be
reduced steadily to the vanishing point. Thus
wherever such a man is at work, wherever such a
man is at play, there the rule of God is at hand.

But that is not enough. Such a man is a member
of his society. He is intimately involved in the
network of impersonal social relations that influence his life and which to some extent he also
influences. It is easy to fall into the error of saying
that as an individual he is helpless, insignificant;

he cannot possibly wield sufficient influence to
make a difference. But is this true? In one of
Petrarch's letters appear these words:

> When a word must be spoken to further a
> good cause, and those whom it behooves to
> speak remain silent, anybody ought to raise his
> voice, and break a silence which may be fraught
> with evil. . . . Many a time a few simple words
> have helped further the welfare of the nation,
> no matter who uttered them; the voice itself dis-
> playing its latent powers, sufficed to move the
> hearts of men.[1]

Let us apply what is suggested here in just one
point of relatedness for the individual; namely,
civic responsibility. Every citizen in our society,
theoretically at any rate, has the ballot. The ballot
represents one available point of attack upon the
impersonal social forces summarized as the state.
Central, therefore, to the individual's social witness is the exercise of the ballot. If a man regards

[1] *Correspondence in Old Age.*

his obligation to use his ballot as an expression of the central commitment of his life, then he will bring to bear upon this function the most comprehensive knowledge and wisdom which he possesses. At the point of the ballot, the individual practices his personal responsibility for the state of which he is a part. Thus, and to that extent, does civic character become synonymous with religious character.

This is a mighty area for the witness. One of the great despairs of our times is the way in which the large-scale nature of the operations of the modern state takes from the ordinary man any responsibility for the state beyond the payment of taxes and service in the armed forces. This withdrawal of responsibility from the individual depersonalizes him. With the loss of a sense of responsibility there has been a corresponding stifling of free social initiative and a destruction of any sense of the future. We are surrounded by a climate of fear; fear of communism; fear of democracy; fear of one another; and fear of tomorrow. The task of

the religious man in whom there is a reigning sense
of his own worth validated for him by the
dynamics of his religious experience is to reinject
into the state the sense of responsibility *to* the individual. The most effective weapon in his hands in
this regard is the ballot itself. Of course this
involves him in many compromises—but he sees
concurrently that no man lives in a society of
which he does not fully approve without some
measure of compromise. His choice is to be indif-
ferent to the state, as if it were no concern of his
or to be involved in the struggle of making the
state more and more sensitive to persons. It is
important to remember that this presupposes that
the individual will seek to align himself with those
persons who are moved by the same dynamics
which influence his life. Among the many com-
binations of associations with persons with which
he becomes involved, the most logical one consistent with his religious insights would be a
religious fellowship. For the Christian such a fellowship is the church. The church thus becomes

the organism fed by the springs of individual and
collective religious experience through which the
Christian works in society. To what extent is this
characteristic of the church? It is obvious that if
the church is to be the most important vehicle giving social character to the Christian individual's
witness, then what the church seeks to achieve in
society it must not foster within its own boundary.
Let us now examine the church in the light of this
social obligation and responsibility.

The central figure of the Christian Church is
Jesus Christ. Even the most casual reading of the
story of his life in the Gospels reveals that central
to his religious experience was his encounter with
God. When Jesus prayed, he was conscious of the
fact that in his prayer he met Somebody, and that
Somebody he called God, Father, Creator. For him
there were two principals in the religious experience, God and man; God and Jesus. It was his
insistence that all men are children of God, and
therefore stand in immediate candidacy for that
experience. It was from within the moving energy

of that experience that he lived, thought, func-
tioned, died. The relevancy of the individual personality took primacy from the meaning of his
religious experience whether he was dealing with
the woman at the well, or Mary, the sister of
Lazarus; whether he was dealing with the rich
young ruler, or the maniac in the desert; whether
he was dealing with the officer in the Roman army,
or Simon Peter, the simple fisherman. The clue to
his behavior was always the same, the significance
of the individual personality and its needs. In one
of his broadest and most audacious thrusts, he says
that even the sacred institution itself is the servant
of the needs of the individual. If we summarize
his meaning at this point, we would say that he
placed before the world, as a creative and dedicated son of Israel, the vision of a great dynamic
ideal in which all peoples were involved as children of God. He suggested the vehicle or tech-
nique by means of which the ideal itself may be
implemented in the common life and experience
of the children of men, the vehicle which is forever

identified with his name and symbolic of his spirit
—love. He placed at the disposal of the individual
children of men a resource, available to each of
them, upon which they may draw for strength and
power to enable them and to sustain them in the
great enterprise of living on such terms. He labeled
this power God. Of such is what I may call the
Jesus idea.

The way the mind makes its initial contact with
ideas is as varied as it is miraculous. Sometimes
the idea comes as a poignant quivering deep within
the cells of the brain; sometimes it comes as a
distinct current of enthusiasm, sweeping all before
it; sometimes it comes as the total response of the
personality to the impact of some impressions and
challenging demand. However the contact is initi-
ated, the profound order remains the same—conception, growth, birth, and development.

The conception is accomplished when the idea
takes on an individual character and a dimension
of self-consciousness in the mind. It separates itself
gradually from other related ideas and then re-

unites itself with them on its own terms. Thus its uniqueness is guaranteed and underscored. Slowly it begins the long journey of growth by creating in the mind new levels of curiosity, fresh contacts with old sources, and sometimes defining all activities of the personality in terms useful to its ends. It is a wonderful sensation—to feel the growth of an idea in the mind.

There comes a moment when the idea has to become objective; when it has to establish an independent life. The person into whose mind it first stirred has to relate himself to it as one who must win the right to be related to it. At such a time, the idea secures its own external form, struggles for place, significance, and status in a highly competitive atmosphere, in an environment that is not under control. It is at this point that the genius of the idea comes into its own, by being a rallying point for all who see in it the meaning of their own hopes and the significance of their own strivings. The moments are perilous, too, because the idea in its "for instanced" form often attracts

those who would destroy it because it threatens or
challenges or even becomes destructive to other
forms regarded as worthful. The story of the conception, growth, birth, and development of an
idea is one with the miracle of life itself.

It is in order now at last to raise the question: Is
the witness of the church in our society the unfold-
ing of such an idea as we see manifested in the
religious experience and the life of Jesus? Whatever may be the delimiting character of the histori-
cal development of the church, the simple fact
remains that at the present moment in our society,
as an institution, the church is divisive and discriminating, even within its fellowship. It is
divided into dozens of splinters. This would
indicate that it is essentially sectarian in character.
As an institution there is no such thing as the
church. There has to be some kind of church.

In other words the church as a social institution
is "adjectival." When I was visiting on the campus
of a university in North India, I asked an Indian
Christian student, "How many students are en-

rolled in this University?" His reply was very informative. He said, "Let me see. There are x number of Anglicans, x number of Baptists, x number of Northern Methodists, English Congregationalists, American Congregationalists, etc." He knew that my concern as a Christian would be the Christian enrollment, and within that concern there was a still more exclusive concern—the kind of Christian by designation. He was amazed to discover that my question was a literal one. I wanted to know the total enrollment of the institution. The concept of denominationalism seems to me to be in itself a violation of what I am delineating as the Jesus idea. The separate vision of a denomination *tends* to give to the individual who embraces it an ultimate, particularized status, even before God; as one of the older men in my boyhood church who admonished me because I was attending too many activities in the Methodist church: "Sometimes," he said, "I think that I am a Baptist first and a Christian second." In our moments of profoundest sobriety, there is clear

recognition of the contradiction that is inherent in
the concept of denominationalism as it is examined
in the light of what for Christianity is the Jesus
idea. Inasmuch as the individual brings to his
religious experience his context, it is perfectly
natural and mandatory that he will enter his
religious experience with his particular denominational frame of reference. That is the door through
which he enters. In the encounter with God in the
religious experience, however, the denominational
frame of reference receives its true status, which
is a *frame of reference,* without standing, as such,
in the ultimate meaning of the experience itself.
To make the frame of reference which is merely
symbolic take on the life-giving character of the
experience itself and thereby become binding as a
principle of discrimination in the wider context
of living and experiencing is to blaspheme against
the experience itself. This, in my judgment, tends
to undermine the integrity of the church as the
promoter and inspirer of religious experience.

But when the church, even within the framework of the principle of discrimination inherent in denominationalism, further delimits itself in terms of class and race, it tends to become an instrument of violence to the religious experience. Here we come upon the shame of what is meant by the phrase of a certain minister in referring to the eleven o'clock hour on Sunday morning as "the great and sacred hour of segregation."

Many years ago when I was doing work in religious education in Roanoke, Virginia, I came one Sunday afternoon to the young people's meeting. Upon arrival, I noticed that the meeting had started and a very tall, rather striking man was making a speech. I wondered who he was and how he got on the program without my knowing anything about it. Most of my questions were answered by what he was saying as I took my seat. "I am a Moslem," he said, "and I come from West Africa. When I realized this afternoon that I had two or three hours to wait for my train connection, I decided that I would visit some Christian church. I walked rather aimlessly from the station and

found myself in front of a large church. I went in.
There was some meeting going on. I was told that
this was not the church for which I was looking;
that the church I wanted was down the other end
of the street in another part of town. It was to this
church that I was directed. I come here and I find
you. You are members of the same denomination as
that other church. Allah laughs aloud in his
Moslem heaven when he beholds the Christian
spectacle of the Christian church white and the
Christian church colored." Without wanting to
create any mood of self-consciousness on the part
of the reader, I would like to quote a paragraph
from *The Protestant Church and the Negro*. This
paragraph gives a very clear picture of the situation.

There are approximately 8,000,000 Protestant
Negroes. About 7,500,000 are in separate Negro
denominations. Therefore, from the local church
through the regional organizations to the national assemblies over 93 per cent of the Negroes

are without association in work and worship
with Christians of other races except in inter-
denominational organizations which involve a
few of their leaders. The remaining 500,000
Negro Protestants—about 6 per cent—are in
predominantly white denominations, and of
these 500,000 Negroes in "white" churches, at
least 99 per cent, judging by the surveys of six
denominations, are in segregated congregations.
They are in association with their white denominational brothers only in national assemblies,
and, in some denominations, in regional, state,
or more local jurisdictional meetings. There
remains a handful of Negro members in local
"white" churches. How many? Call it one-tenth
of one per cent of all the Negro Protestant
Christians in the United States—8,000 souls—
the figure is probably much too large. Whatever
the figure actually is, the number of white and
Negro persons who ever gather together for
worship under the auspices of Protestant Christianity is almost microscopic. And where inter-

racial worship does occur, it is, for the most part, in communities where there are only a few Negro families and where, therefore, only a few Negro individuals are available to "white" churches.

The author continues with this paragraph:

The same pattern appears to be true for other colored minorities, that is, Japanese, Chinese, Indians, Mexicans, Puerto Ricans. Regarding the Mexicans and Puerto Ricans, for example, a director of home missions work in a great denomination says his experience leads him to believe that "generally there is little, if any, discrimination here though in a community which has a large Mexican population it is quite true that they have their own churches." [2]

Once again let us be reminded that the individual brings into his religious experience his frame of reference, with all that that implies. It is

[2] Frank Loescher, *The Protestant Church and the Negro*, Association Press, 1948, 76 ff.

the door through which he enters into the experience of contact, fellowship, communion, with God.
What he experiences *there* must have a quality of
intrinsic significance that transcends the frame of
reference or his context. If, however, the frame of
reference is one which by social definition pre-
cludes him from sharing in the availability of the
religious experience under auspices other than
those that are unique to his frame of reference,
then the frame of reference, in and of itself,
becomes coextensive with the religious experience.

*The ideal that is fundamental to the Jesus idea,
as we have defined it, is a vision of all men as children of God and the church as a social institution
formally entrusted with this idea in our society
cannot withhold it from any man because of status,
of class, of any social definition whatsoever. A part
of its instrumentality in society is to a commitment
of attack on any binding social classification that
takes precedence over the intrinsic worthfulness of
the individual as embodied in the centrality of the
religious experience.*

But there is a still more profound question at issue here. Is the religious experience as defined uniquely Christian or is it more universal in character? If in the religious experience a man identifies Jesus rather than God as the other principal in his religious experience, then the *exclusive* character of the religious experience becomes undeniable. In my judgment this raises more questions than it solves because it places the most fundamental moment in the life of the individual at the disposal of only those persons who bring to the moment a certain body of formal beliefs. Such a position establishes on theological and metaphysical grounds a *principle of separateness* in the human family that paves the way for the promulgation in the world of a Cult of Inequality that puts man against man and group against group. If such a cult is rooted in an experience so profound, as the religious experience is, then the metaphysical purpose that such an experience generates becomes a banner under which all manner of brutality and human misery may march.

But if in the religious experience the other principal is God, who is sensed as Creator of life and Father of the human spirit, then at such a moment the individual stands on his intrinsic worthfulness as a human being and affirms in the integrity of the moment his solidarity with all mankind.

The character then of a social institution whose inspiration is rooted in its commitment to that kind of religious experience becomes more and more defined in activities, functions, social attitudes, that defy all class, group, or ethnic affiliation. The startling words of Jesus come to life again. "For whosoever shall do the will of my Father which is in heaven, the same is my brother, and sister, and mother" (Matthew 12:50).

One may raise the question: Is it practicable to envision such a possibility for the church as a social institution? Ten years ago my answer would have been "No." During this decade it has been my inspiringly heartbreaking privilege to test in a limited way the validity of such a concept, in sharing in the development of the Church for the Fellowship of All Peoples in San Francisco.

From the beginning we were seeking some quality of experience that could quarantine the sense of separateness that divided men into groups so that it would not continue to invade and become operative in the area of human relations. Upon examination it was found that it is quite possible to have experiences of unity with other human beings, which experiences seem to undercut the sense of separateness at all levels, except that of personal individuality. In my own life I have had such authentic experiences that have seemed to be one with the integrating quality of the religious encounter. If a man could have such experiences in which increasing numbers of his fellows were involved with him, then such experiences would be more compelling and controlling in his relations with them, than the things which separate or divide. It was our hope that a church could be projected on the basis of the continuing validity of the kind of religious experience that would be uniting and integrating. Thus such an experience would become more and more a creative attack on segregation by broadening and extending the boundaries of any sense of separateness until they included more and more members of the human race without regard to social or creedal status. Think of it! A religious fellowship in which the central emphasis would be the worship of God in whose Presence men and women of whatever pattern of living and orientation might be merged into increasing moments of inclusiveness. Conceivably, such a religious fellowship would inspire and sustain the kind of program in which at the level of activity and function experiences of unity would be more compelling than the concepts, the habit patterns, the prejudices, and the beliefs that divide. In my thought and with my particular background, such a fellowship would be defined by me as being Christian.

It is not my purpose to tell the story of such a venture, but merely to bear witness to the fact that it is a reasonable thing, even in a society pre-

disposed toward segregation and separateness as
is our society, for such a church with such a commitment to relate the religious experience to the
social witness. It is only such a religious experience
as this that can hope to generate the kind of energy
to sustain the kind of ethic that has always been
and now is the dream of men of good will in every
age and in every culture and of diverse faiths. It is
only such a religious experience that can give to
mankind a time-binding and, therefore, *timeless*
basis for integrated action; that can inspire a willingness to sacrifice, even life itself, on behalf of
its fulfillment in the commonweal; and that can
give to the least significant or the most prestige-
bearing individual a sense of participating in a
collective destiny in which the whole human race
is involved. It is in this dimension that the social
witness has to be sustained by the religious experience.

Man builds his little shelter, he raises his little
wall; man builds his little altar, he worships his
little God; man organizes the resources of his little

life, he defends his little barrier. All this—to no avail! What man is committed to in the religious experience which is the insight of these pages is this: The effective possibility of a vital religious fellowship [3] which is so creative in character, so convincing in quality that it inspires the mind to multiply experiences of unity—which experiences of unity become over and over and over again more compelling than the concepts, the ways of life, the sects, and the creeds that separate men. It is my belief that in the Presence of God there is neither male nor female, white nor black, Gentile nor Jew, Protestant nor Catholic, Hindu, Buddhist, nor Moslem, but a human spirit stripped to the literal substance of itself before God. Wherever man has this sense of the Eternal in his spirit, he hunts for it in his home, in his work, among his friends, in his pleasures, and in all the levels of his function. It is my simple faith that this is the kind of universe that sustains that kind of adventure,

[3] It is not my claim that the Church for the Fellowship of All Peoples is such a vital religious fellowship but that it is feeling and believing its way toward that goal.

and what we see dimly now in the churning confusion and chaos of our tempestuous times will someday be the common experience of all the children of men everywhere.

These pages are reserved for the reader to use in whatever way his or her own creative encounter may suggest.

116 RW 2 engines

11 Eph 3 on true 7 Fr

118-119 (1 pg. before) on Mt. 10 ¹² disciple
14 ✳ taken notes on their focus

Let 1 "divine nature" Eckhart p 43

84 Rom 12:1-2
see 9 ch 2

USe 22 II Red Sermon - th virtue
next sun also 11 Forthwith - punali"

Pret ought to go out to see th Weep

5314 Cast your burden on the
I SoS